THREE-DIMENSIONAL
INTEGRATED CIRCUIT LAYOUT

ANDREW HARTER
Corpus Christi College
Universtity of Cambridge

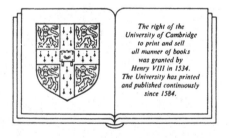

The right of the
University of Cambridge
to print and sell
all manner of books
was granted by
Henry VIII in 1534.
The University has printed
and published continuously
since 1584.

CAMBRIDGE UNIVERSITY PRESS

Cambridge

New York Port Chester Melbourne Sydney

CAMBRIDGE UNIVERSITY PRESS
Cambridge, New York, Melbourne, Madrid, Cape Town, Singapore, São Paulo, Delhi

Cambridge University Press
The Edinburgh Building, Cambridge CB2 8RU, UK

Published in the United States of America by Cambridge University Press, New York

www.cambridge.org
Information on this title: www.cambridge.org/9780521118163

First published 1991
This digitally printed version 2009

A catalogue record for this publication is available from the British Library

ISBN 978-0-521-41630-6 hardback
ISBN 978-0-521-11816-3 paperback

Additional resources for this publication at www.cambridge.org/9780521118163

To my parents

Abstract

Some recent developments in semiconductor process technology have made possible the construction of three-dimensional integrated circuits. Unlike other technological developments in two-dimensional integration, these circuits present a new and inherently richer connection topology. This offers the potential for improved layout in terms of increased density and reduced interconnect length. These circuits will be difficult and expensive to manufacture, at least in the short term, and the scale of the improvement in layout is not apparent. This dissertation presents a discussion of layout and design for three-dimensional integrated circuits.

A number of materials and techniques can be used in the manufacture of such circuits. This choice has a profound bearing on the topology of circuit layout. A classification relating process technology to layout topology is developed and illustrated with the design of a number of circuits. A layout system is presented as the vehicle for a series of experiments in three-dimensional layout. It is shown that the system can be constrained to perform circuit layout in a number of topologies in the classification.

Finally, some attempt to quantify the benefits of three-dimensional layout is made. The layout model is calibrated by designing examples of basic circuit elements. This is done using a set of design rules corresponding to a proposed three-dimensional process technology. Circuit layouts produced by the system are compared with conventional two-dimensional layouts, and the variation in layout quality as a function of the three-dimensionality of a layout is explored.

Preface

I am indebted to my supervisor, Andy Hopper, for his encouragement and support. He first introduced me to the topic of computer aided design of integrated circuits when I was an undergraduate, and has been a source of guidance ever since. I am also indebted to Roger Needham for extending the facilities of the Computer Laboratory. I am grateful that both Andy and Roger have demonstrated quite remarkable patience. The Science and Engineering Research Council provided funding for three years for which I am thankful.

Of the many people who have been a source of help, I would particularly like to thank David Wheeler for a number of stimulating discussions, and Haroon Ahmed of the Microcircuit Engineering Laboratory for introducing me to the technology of three-dimensional circuits. Alan Mathewson and Ciaran Cahill, of the National Microelectronics Research Centre, University College, Cork, have contributed to my further understanding of the technological possibilities. Elements of the systems used in the case study described in chapter two were developed by myself, Jeremy Dion, Alan Jones, Tony Mann, Trevor Morris, John Porter, Peter Robinson and Chris Stenton. I would like to thank Tony Mann and John Porter for reminding me about the details of the placement and routing schemes.

Chris Stenton and Steve Temple have contributed many helpful suggestions particularly in the experimental stages and were diligent proof readers, as were Tim Cole and David Greaves. I am grateful for their suggestions for improvements.

This dissertation is the result of my own work and is not the outcome of any work done in collaboration. I declare that this dissertation is not the same as any other dissertation I have submitted for a degree, diploma or other qualification at any university. Furthermore, no part of this dissertation has been or is currently being submitted for any such qualification.

Contents

List of Figures

List of Plates

These illustrations are available in colour as a download from
www.cambridge.org/9780521118163

List of Tables

List of Algorithms

Glossary of Terms

The number of the page on which the term is introduced appears in parentheses after each term.

FET	Field-effect transistor (4).
MOS	Metal-oxide-semiconductor (4).
NMOS	n-type metal-oxide-semiconductor (4).
PMOS	p-type metal-oxide-semiconductor (4).
CMOS	Complementary-metal-oxide-semiconductor (5).
CAD	Computer-aided design (5).
SRAM	Static random-access memory (5).
DRAM	Dynamic random-access memory (11).
SSI	Small-scale integration (11).
MSI	Medium-scale integration (11).
LSI	Large-scale integration (11).
VLSI	Very-large-scale integration (11).
WSI	Wafer-scale integration (11).
FIFO	First-in first-out (20).
HDL	Hardware Description Language (24).

CFR	Cambridge Fast Ring (28).
ASIC	Application Specific Integrated Circuit (29).
SOI	Silicon on insulator (35).
CVD	Chemical Vapour Deposition (38).

Chapter 1

Introduction

1.1   Thesis aims

A study of three-dimensional integrated circuit layout is presented in this dissertation. Three-dimensional integrated circuits are those in which active devices such as transistors are fabricated in each of at least two vertically stacked semiconducting planes. An evaluation of the potential benefits of using three-dimensional integration is carried out. Such benefits include greater layout densities, shorter interconnection lengths and faster circuits. Emphasis is placed on considering the layout methods required to use three-dimensional fabrication techniques and to accrue the above benefits.

Three-dimensional circuits are one of a number of recent developments in integrated circuit construction techniques to have stimulated interest. Other developments include the use of a variety of semiconductor and wiring materials for faster transistors and connections, and enhanced processing techniques to improve yield and reduce transistor geometries. This enables both physically larger and logically more complex circuits to be integrated. These developments do not present any new layout problems. The search for better, more automated layout continues independently of such technological advances. The same is not true in the three-dimensional domain. The juxtaposition of devices in three dimensions presents an inherently different set of connection properties to the two-dimensional case, since a device may now have neighbours above and below in addition to those in the semiconducting plane. Layout in three dimensions requires new techniques to fully exploit this property.

1

Since three-dimensional fabrication techniques were first demonstrated in the early eighties [Gibbons 80], two areas of research have been explored. The primary research has concentrated on the necessary fabrication techniques. In the main, such work has not considered any of the broader issues of layout. The other research has been of a theoretical nature, using graph theory to put bounds on the expected reduction in interconnection length in three-dimensional layouts. A primary goal of the work described here is to present a quantitative measurement of the efficacy of three-dimensional circuit layout. This involves a comparison of two and three-dimensional layouts for several classes of circuit, and represents an approach somewhere between the two mentioned above. In order to perform such a comparison, three-dimensional layout algorithms have been developed to operate within a framework which allows the definition of a number of topologies. The topologies can be mapped against the constraints which different three-dimensional devices impose, such as the number of device layers and the availability and distribution of connections.

1.2   Thesis structure

The remainder of this chapter introduces two-dimensional chip technology. Beginning with a brief history of key developments in the manufacture of integrated circuits and continuing with the description of a typical two-dimensional fabrication sequence, the chapter concludes with a discussion of some of the recent trends in fabrication technology. This provides a background for the description of three-dimensional fabrication presented later. Chapter two is a discourse on two-dimensional chip design, highlighting the need for abstraction and automation in the design process. Gate array, standard cell and custom design are introduced and compared as possible integration routes. A framework for the classification of elements of design automation is introduced and used to describe a selection of design tools. Chapter two concludes with a case study detailing the design and implementation of a circuit in gate array and standard cell formats.

The remaining chapters are devoted to three-dimensional integration. Chapter three contains details of the techniques enabling three-dimensional devices to be constructed and of some of the devices which have been created. Included at this point is a discussion of the technological difficulties of constructing three-dimensional circuits. Chapter four concerns three-dimensional structures in a more abstract sense. A classification is introduced which maps combinations of the technological constraints of three-dimensional circuits into groups of layout topologies. This enables the effect of a technological constraint to be seen in the composition of the resulting structure. Also included at this point is a review of other work on three-dimensional layout.

Chapter five describes a model for experiments in three-dimensional layout. The model introduces cells of homogeneous size, shape and connection interface. The purpose of modelling layout with such specific cells is to explore the possibilities of connection by direct cell abutment, a popular technique in many two-dimensional layouts. Included at this point is the practical design of cells satisfying the required geometric properties of abutting cells. Chapter six contains details of the construction of a highly configurable experimental layout system based on the above model. Descriptions of the layout algorithms and merit functions which were developed are given, and the difficulties and limitations encountered are discussed.

Chapters seven and eight present the results from a large number of experiments carried out with a wide range of circuits and parameter values. The results are scaled with dimensions extracted from the cells designed earlier. In chapter seven, the configuration options of the system are examined. In chapter eight, the effect of varying the number and composition of layers on the quality of layout is presented. Also included for comparison are results from two-dimensional circuit layouts. Chapter nine contains concluding remarks and suggestions for further research.

1.3   Two-dimensional chip technology

1.3.1   A brief history of integration

The concept of the integrated circuit was first proposed by G.W.A. Dummer in 1952. He imagined a solid block containing layers of insulating, conducting and amplifying material with electrical functions being directly connected by cutting out areas on the various layers. At the time he had no idea how this could be realised. Transistor technology was still in its infancy, the first germanium bipolar transistor working in 1947. A number of advances in materials and processing technology prevailed before the integration imagined by Dummer was achieved. Four key developments were the controlled growth of high purity single crystal semiconductors, the understanding of semiconductor doping by the diffusion of impurities, the development of methods for selectively etching materials and the use of patterned insulating layers to mask the diffusion process.

The first functional integrated circuit was demonstrated and patented by J. Kilby in 1959. It consisted of a slice of single crystal germanium containing a bipolar transistor, a capacitor and three resistors. It demonstrated how several components could be integrated on the same semiconductor, but did not show any satisfactory method of connecting the components, this being achieved by hand using thin gold wires. The planar process, initially developed by J. Hoerni and R. Noyce in 1959 as an improved method of manufacturing discrete silicon transistors, combined the existing diffusion and masking techniques with a method of connection. A final layer of patterned oxide was used as a mask for connections between regions of the transistor and the outside world. Connections could then be formed by the deposition of aluminium in a batch production method. The techniques of the planar process when applied to the manufacture of integrated circuits caused a revolution in the electronics industry.

One of the first commercially available planar integrated circuits was a flip-flop containing four transistors and five resistors. It was one of a family of resistor-transistor logic chips offered by Fairchild in 1961. In 1964 the first linear integrated circuit was developed by R. Wildar, an operational amplifier called the μA702 which contained twelve transistors and five resistors. It was remarkable not only for being the first operational amplifier on a single chip, but also for the ingenuity of the design. Rather than attempting to translate a discrete circuit into silicon, Wildar thought in terms of the properties of the silicon components themselves. Where possible, he used DC biased transistors instead of resistors, and relied on matching component characteristics, only assuming approximate absolute values. Still in manufacture, the μA702 is the longest surviving integrated circuit to date. Transistor-transistor logic emerged as the permanent successor to resistor-transistor logic in 1964 with the advent of the Texas Instruments 5400 digital logic family.

For much of the decade or so between the invention of the transistor and the integrated circuit, research was directed at improving the characteristics and manufacturing techniques of bipolar devices. The perfection of the planar process solved many of the problems, and generated a new impetus in the experimentation with new devices. One such device was the field-effect transistor (FET). The first FETs had an aluminium gate insulated by a silicon dioxide layer from the underlying semiconductor channel, and the term metal-oxide-semiconductor (MOS) or MOS-FET was coined. In general, a MOS transistor is slower but smaller, cheaper and requires less power than a bipolar transistor. The first MOS integrated circuit, devised by S.R. Hofstein and F.P. Heiman in 1962, provided general purpose logic functions and contained sixteen transistors. MOS transistors can be constructed with either electrons as the majority carriers (NMOS) or holes (PMOS).

Integrated circuits combining both types of MOS transistor, complementary-metal-oxide-semiconductor (CMOS), can be arranged to consume even less power but require an increased number of processing steps. Demonstrated in 1963, they were available commercially in 1968.

By that time, the techniques of integrated circuit manufacture were maturing, and the pace of integration measured in terms of increased transistor count, greater manufacturing yield and reduced cost was marked. Finally, from a time roughly a decade after the development of the integrated circuit, three landmark designs deserve mention. First, the Micromosaic chip made by Fairchild in 1967 was a double innovation. It was the first gate array, that is a chip containing a number of unconnected logic gates in fixed positions which can be joined by specifying the pattern of the final layer of connections. It also involved the first use of computer-aided design (CAD) to translate a description of the customer's circuit into the necessary pattern for the connections. The second chip was the first sizeable integrated semiconductor memory, the Fairchild 4100 designed by H.T. Chua in 1970. Containing 256 bits of static random-access memory (SRAM) constructed from fast bipolar transistors, the chip was used extensively in the ILLIAC IV, one of the first mainframe computers to have a fully integrated primary store. The third chip was the first microprocessor, the Intel 4004 designed by M.E. Hoff in 1971. The four bit processor was part of the design for a series of calculators for a Japanese company. The processor contained an adder, an accumulator, sixteen four bit registers and a push down stack. The 4004, however, did not just appear in calculators, but opened whole new worldwide markets. Further details of the history of integrated circuits can be found in [Braun 82], [Atherton 83], [Augarten 83] and [Dummer 83].

1.3.2   A fabrication sequence

Some key elements of the planar process applied to the fabrication of a silicon MOS transistor are illustrated in Figure 1.1. Semiconductor wafers typically 1mm thick and 100mm in diameter are sliced from a cylindrical ingot of single crystal grown by the seeded annealing of molten polycrystalline silicon. One surface is polished to a mirror like finish with diamond powder (Figure 1.1(a)). A $1\mu m$ thick oxide is grown on the polished surface of the wafer, and this is then coated with photoresist material (Figure 1.1(b)). An ultraviolet light source exposes the photoresist through a wafer sized mask pattern (Figure 1.1(c)), which is then developed to leave areas of exposed oxide which are etched back to the silicon substrate. The undeveloped photoresist is removed (Figure 1.1(d)). Transistors will be created in the areas of

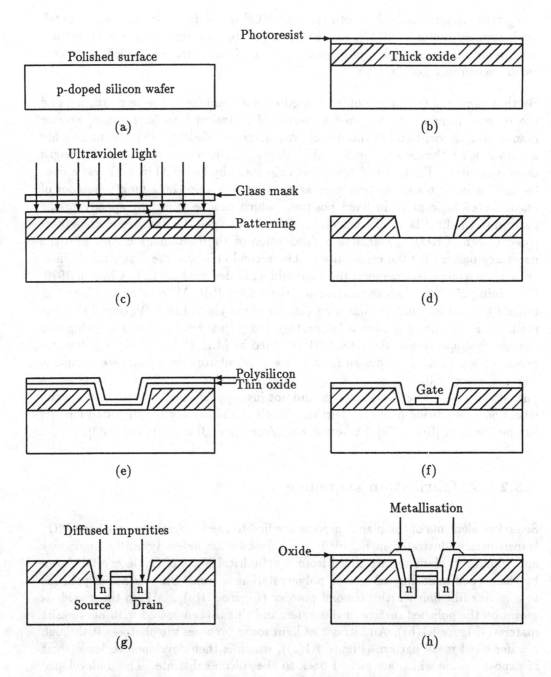

Figure 1.1: A simple fabrication sequence for a MOS transistor

exposed substrate formed by this initial patterning.

A 50nm thin oxide layer is then grown under highly controlled conditions, followed by the chemical vapour deposition of a $1\mu m$ polysilicon layer (Figure 1.1(e)). The polysilicon is patterned and etched, defining the transistor gates (Figure 1.1(f)). The thin oxide is etched away in areas not protected by the polysilicon and the whole structure is exposed to a gaseous source of dopant which diffuses into any exposed silicon. This defines $1\mu m$ deep transistor junctions in the substrate and increases the conductivity of the polysilicon (Figure 1.1(g)). The same mask is therefore used to define both the gate and junction regions, commonly known as a self-aligned process. A further patterned oxide layer opens contact holes to the substrate and polysilicon. These are filled with a layer of aluminium which is patterned to provide interconnect (Figure 1.1(h)).

1.4 Trends in integration

1.4.1 Faster and denser circuits

From the outset there has been demand from the electronics industry for faster and more highly integrated circuits. Chip manufacturers have responded with an approximate doubling in transistor count per device every year, often referred to as Moore's Law, and an increase in speed by a factor of one and a half every year. These trends arise from the desire to reduce the weight, bulk, power consumption and cost of integrated systems, while increasing the speed, manufacturability and ease of assembly. The communications and computer industries embody these trends. At each level of increased capacity, new applications present themselves and so the demand persists.

The limit on the number of transistors in an integrated circuit is largely an economic one, relating to the cost per working circuit. This cost rises when the number of working circuits per cm^2 of wafer falls. This is principally caused by a reduction in manufacturing yield, which is the number of working circuits as a percentage of the number of circuits manufactured. Circuits so large as to have a yield of less than 25% are unlikely to be economic to manufacture in quantity, and circuits with a yield of 1% are unlikely to be manufactured at all. In general, circuits fail to work when critical regions such as the gate and channel areas of a transistor, the contacts between connections and transistors or the connections themselves coincide with some structural fault. Such faults may be inherent in the materials involved, introduced by the processing techniques employed or caused by lithographic or mask alignment inaccuracies. Considering the maximum cost per working circuit to be invariant, there are three ways to increase the number of devices per circuit. First, device geometries can be reduced thereby increasing the device density. Second, fabrication technology can be improved to reduce defect density and thereby permit larger areas to be used. Third, techniques can be employed to prevent defects from causing the circuit to malfunction.

The limit on the switching speed of transistors in an integrated circuit is governed by the electron mobility of the semiconductor and the capacitances on the conducting path of the signal which is switching. Materials with a range of mobilities are used, and the choice of semiconductor material has a profound effect on the performance of the circuit. Capacitances are reduced by scaling down dimensions. The corresponding increase in circuit density also reduces interconnect length. Finally, at the system level, larger scale integration implies fewer chips, fewer connections between chips and less delay in input and output buffering and signal propagation.

1.4.2   Enhanced processing

The basic process described earlier suffers from a number of disadvantages which make it unsuitable for very small geometry devices (Figure 1.2). Transistor separation S is limited to around $1\mu m$ due to the lateral diffusion of the source and drain implanted regions under the thick oxide. Poor surface planarisation during gate oxide deposition leads to thinning of the photoresist at the channel/thick oxide step and possible gate disconnection, and a minimum channel width W of around $3\mu m$ is necessary. A number of enhanced processing sequences have been proposed to avoid such problems and to achieve smaller geometries and device spacing. Separations of $0.5\mu m$ and channel widths of $1.5\mu m$ are reported [Tsai 88].

Creation of smaller features also requires better lithography and alignment between mask steps. Conventional ultraviolet light step and repeat lithography is capable of defining channel lengths L down to about $1.5\mu m$. This limit is imposed by the wavelength of the light, diffraction at the edge of mask patterns and alignment tolerances. Direct write electron beam lithography is capable of much finer geometries down to $0.15\mu m$ [Fichtner 82], and incorporates the flexibility to write different designs on a single wafer. However, the serial scanning nature of the beam makes throughput very low. X-ray or X-ray/photo lithography offers the best combination of high resolution and throughput with a line width of $0.2\mu m$ being reported [Mikaye 87].

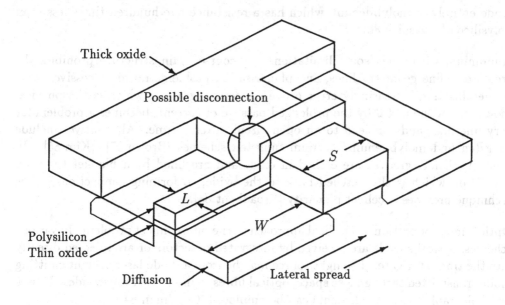

Figure 1.2: Problems with small geometry transistors

1.4.3   Alternative materials

There are alternative materials for the semiconducting, gate and wiring elements
of integrated circuits. Of the various materials with semiconducting properties,
gallium arsenide has the greatest potential for high performance. This is due to a
high electron mobility, roughly an order of magnitude greater than that of silicon.
Bulk gallium arsenide is also available in a semi-insulating form giving good device
isolation, and reducing parasitic capacitances. The manufacture of gallium arsenide
transistors is, however, subject to more complex and highly controlled processing
due largely to the more stringent conditions required for correct transistor operation.

For the gate layer, polysilicon has a high resistance which limits its usefulness as
a level of interconnect away from the gate region. In general, it is unsuitable for
long distances, critical signals or power tracks. Refractory metals show promise as a
gate and interconnect material either when compounded with silicon or in elemental
form. Both polysilicon and diffusion can be capped with a titanium disilicide layer
formed by depositing titanium and then performing a rapid thermal anneal. Requiring no extra mask steps, this process reduces the effective resistance of polysilicon
and diffusion by a factor of fifty [Lai 86]. Alternatively, the gate material can be

made entirely of molybdenum, which has a resistance five hundred times less than polysilicon [Kwasnick 88].

Aluminium wiring has some limitations. A course grain structure prohibits the creation of fine geometry lines, and planarisation problems make successive layers of metallisation increasingly error prone. Electromigration, which is the physical movement of the metal by the prolonged passage of current, becomes a problem for very fine lines and can lead to an open circuit after a time. Alternatives include tungsten and molybdenum/titanium tungsten schemes [Brown 87], [Kim 85]. In a novel scheme, grooves are etched in oxide and are filled by a blanket tungsten deposition which is then etched back to the oxide, so forming connections. This technique provides excellent planarity [Broadbent 88].

Optical interconnection is a radical approach to the interconnect problem. In various schemes, optical signals are received by integrated detectors or are injected directly into the transistor gate. The light source may be from a diode laser or light emitting diode transmitted through free space, optical fibres or integrated waveguides. Lenses and holographic routing elements can be employed [Goodman 84].

1.4.4   Mixed technologies

Bipolar and FET technologies have different speed, power consumption and current drive properties. They are frequently used together in systems containing separate bipolar and FET transistors, and it is natural to consider monolithic combination. The most mature and successful combination is of bipolar and CMOS, leading to the BiCMOS technology. This has an increased speed and drive capacity both for off-chip connections and between functions in the integrated circuit. Bipolar transistors are usually fabricated in an epitaxial silicon layer, that is a layer of silicon grown on a silicon wafer. The epitaxial layer is of controlled thickness and with precise levels of homogeneously distributed dopant. A number of selectively grown epitaxial layers can be used in BiCMOS circuits to optimise the doping and thickness of the active regions in each type of transistor [Washio 87], [O 88].

Of the many applications for BiCMOS technology, microprocessor design shows great potential since many of the standard functional elements of a processor benefit from performance in their output stages. A BiCMOS cell library containing adders, multipliers, read only and content addressable memory cells is reported which can be combined to form a processor roughly twice as fast as the CMOS equivalent [Hotta 88]. Such BiCMOS cells are larger than the CMOS counterparts and a speed/space tradeoff must be made. Short, low fan-out local connections can be driven directly by CMOS cells, while longer, higher capacitance global connections benefit from the drive capability of bipolar output stages in BiCMOS cells. Semiconductor memories also benefit greatly from BiCMOS technology, and a 1Mbit BiCMOS dynamic random-access memory (DRAM) is reported in [Kobayashi 89].

The monolithic co-integration of gallium arsenide and silicon transistors is a recent novel development [Shichijo 88]. First, a silicon wafer is prefabricated with CMOS transistors. Gallium arsenide FETs are fabricated in material grown epitaxially in 3μm deep wells etched into the silicon substrate. Two metal levels are provided to connect the two device types. The process would in principle support the co-integration of any gallium arsenide technology with any silicon technology. A likely application of this technique is to integrate optoelectronic gallium arsenide devices into CMOS circuits.

1.4.5   Wafer-scale integration

With every increased level of integration, there are major cost reductions and improvements in reliability as the number of discrete packages and external connections in a system is reduced. This has been apparent with small-scale integration (SSI) involving tens of transistors, medium-scale integration (MSI) involving hundreds of transistors, large-scale integration (LSI) involving thousands of transistors and very-large-scale integration (VLSI) involving tens of thousands of transistors and above. As mentioned before, integrated circuits undergo an approximate doubling in functional density every year, but a more modest doubling in chip area every six years [Carlson 86]. Therefore the increase in function is attributable largely to reduced geometries. In the extreme, a monolithic integrated circuit could consume the entire wafer area, and wafer-scale integration (WSI) is the term describing methods used to construct such circuits. One of the key features in WSI is the use of fault tolerance to counteract the yield problems of physically larger integrated circuits.

Fault tolerance requires potentially massive and repeated testing at various stages of fabrication, provision of redundancy and mechanisms for configuration. Testing must not only provide fault detection, but also fault location in order to effect repairs. The circuit requires a high degree of testability, and extra circuitry is added to facilitate this. Redundancy is required to provide spares for the replacement of faulty elements. Granularity of redundancy is an issue, replacement being possible at the transistor, gate or function level. Restructuring techniques involve the addition of links or blowing of fuses in the fabrication stages [Calder 85], [Komano 88]. This is used to isolate the faulty unit and enable a replacement.

Alternatively, restructuring can be achieved by the electrical programming of semi-conductor switches. In this case, a more sophisticated failure tolerance can be implemented, where future faults can also be located and circumvented. In addition, self-testing, self-configurable WSI circuits have been suggested. Amongst the first of these was a square or hexagonal array of self-testing shift register cells which can be configured into a serial memory. During configuration, a spiral chain of cells is built, avoiding cells which fail the self-test [Aubusson 78]. More recently a self-testing, self-configuring wafer containing a 7×7 array of string processing elements has been proposed [Electronics 85b].

The most suitable applications for WSI are systems with repeated regular structures and pipeline or bus-oriented structures. These simplify the redundancy requirements, and reduce the need for additional wiring levels by having simple interconnection at the module level. Large areas of random logic requiring extensive cross wafer communication attract a high redundancy cost and are much less successful. Memory is often seen as the ideal candidate for WSI, and has been the subject of considerable effort. However, the discrete assembly of VLSI memory is a simple matter, and results in a density only half that achievable with the equivalent WSI memory, although the possibility of automatic fault correction is excluded [Carlson 86].

1.4.6 Multichip modules

Traditional hybrid manufacture uses ceramic substrates patterned with relatively course metallisation and populated with conventional wire-bonded chips. Alternatively silicon substrates patterned with fine metallisation and populated with flip-chips bonded with solder bumps have been investigated. This results in a greater density of circuits and better thermal matching of chips and substrate, leading to increased reliability [Spielberger 84]. An added advantage for manufacturers wishing to protect circuit designs is that it also prevents reverse engineering. This silicon-on-silicon packaging of VLSI circuits provides an alternative to WSI which avoids the need for fault tolerance by combining only fully functional, tested chips. Very high densities can be achieved, and VLSI chips with large numbers of pins can be accommodated, permitting a high degree of communication between the chips in the module. Furthermore, connections between chips which are entirely local to the module do not require large, powerful buffers.

Finally, recently discovered high temperature superconductors are serious candidates for system level interconnect [Kwon 87]. Virtually lossless, low propagation delay interconnect with reduced cross section is an attractive property. High temperature in this context means around 100K, a distinct disadvantage for everyday electronics. Note, however, that some supercomputers are already operated at these low temperatures.

1.4.7   Assumptions

Elements of electronic design can be classified as being either analog or digital. Analog circuits operate using a large range of values of some physical quantity such as voltage or current. Analog circuits often model some mathematical function, for example a linear amplifier can be configured to differentiate an input voltage with respect to time. Digital circuits operate using a small number of discrete values of voltage to represent different states. For example, circuits using two voltages to represent '0' and '1' can model boolean logic and systems of binary arithmetic. Digital circuits are, in general, simpler to design and fabricate and unless otherwise stated, integrated circuits are implicitly digital throughout the remainder of this dissertation. Furthermore, where the integrated circuit technology is unspecified it is assumed to be based on MOS rather than bipolar transistors.

Chapter 2

Two-Dimensional Chip Design

2.1 Abstraction and automation

2.1.1 Goals

The goal of the chip design problem is the specification in absolute units of the precise geometric content of each mask in a particular fabrication process, such that the integrated circuits created by the application of the masks exhibit the intended function. This specification forms the interface between the design and fabrication domains. The intersection of shapes in the set of masks characterises the circuit by determining the nature, location and size of devices and wiring. At the final stage the specification will be a stream of data suitable for either driving mask making equipment or controlling a direct write device.

As the scale of integration increases, so does the complexity of the design problem. The huge volumes of data involved stretch to the limit the human capability to specify a functionally correct layout in reasonable time. An individual's ability to conceive a complex design and successfully translate it into the very detailed information required for mask making is doubtful. The introduction of abstraction is an essential element in chip design. Abstraction is the process of symbolising concepts by extracting common qualities from individual cases. The power of computer automation can then be applied to manipulate the symbols of abstractions.

15

2.1.2   Axioms

Properties of materials and devices for a particular process can be derived empirically from observations and measurements made in the fabrication plant. These properties are taken to be axiomatic to the chip design problem. There are two sets of such axioms. The first set describe the properties and behaviour of semiconductor and wiring materials in particular configurations. The properties include the resistance and capacitance of materials of given shape and size and at a higher level things such as transistor gain. The behaviour describes the way in which such properties change with temperature, voltage and incident electromagnetic radiation. These axioms are used to generate models for semiconductor devices which can be used to predict the behaviour of specific arrangements of devices and wiring connections under a range of ambient conditions. For example, the resistance and capacitance of doped polysilicon enables the load of a polysilicon wire of given length and width to be calculated. This in turn enables the edge speed along the wire from a transistor switching at a given supply voltage and operating temperature to be modelled.

The second set of axioms is a collection of geometric design rules to which the patterns on the masks must conform. The rules specify the necessary relationship between the size, shape and separation of features on the masks for the correct construction of transistors, wiring and contacts between the two. The rules are derived from knowledge of the capabilities of the process technology. For example, the minimum line width will be determined by the resolution of the mask making and exposure techniques and etching. Transistor separation will additionally depend on the degree of lateral diffusion in the channel, while the accuracy of mask registration is a primary component of many rules. The more accurately successive masks can be aligned, the smaller the tolerances built into the rules need to be.

2.1.3   Rules

Design rules provide an important abstraction of the physical process into constraints and dependencies which can be combined and checked in an automated fashion. This helps to ensure that the circuit is physically viable, if not logically correct. Design rules are not, however, a means of guaranteeing correct operation. They are a probabilistic statement about the expected yield and circuit function. A set of masks may conform to the design rules and yet may not achieve the desired yield, and working chips without processing defects may not exhibit the required function or performance, despite logically correct design.

The rules embody an attempt to minimise transistor size and maximise circuit density, while also maintaining acceptable yield. Tight rules mean smaller, faster and lower powered chips with more per wafer. However, the nearer the dimensions come to the limitations of the process the greater the chance of circuit failure due to line breaks, line shorts and improperly defined or misaligned regions. In the extreme, the percentage of working chips will be reduced. Conservative rules may lead to an increased percentage of working chips, but they are larger and so the number of working chips per wafer may actually go down.

The most comprehensive scheme defines 'μ rules' which give the minimum feature sizes and separations for each mask in a particular process. This scheme permits the greatest degree of layout optimisation by exploiting special cases. However, the large number of rules is difficult to apply, and historically most design automation has not been sufficiently powerful to manipulate a μ rule based system. Another scheme reduces the number of rules by specifying feature locations in terms of a grid of pitch α and parameterising feature sizes in terms of a constant β (Figure 2.1).

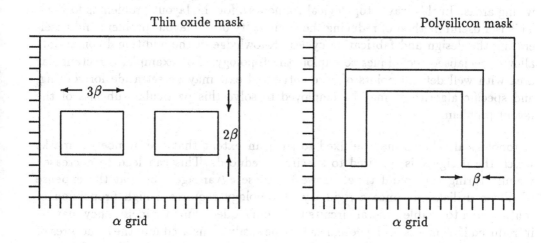

Figure 2.1: An example of '$\alpha\beta$' design rules

A simpler approach popularised by Mead and Conway reduces the number of rules still further [Mead 80]. Normalised or lambda rules rationalise and collapse the constraints of the μ rules in terms of a single parameter λ. This parameter characterises the linear feature or basic length unit in terms of the resolution of the complete process. Such rules are easy to apply and check and are portable, allowing fabrication on a number of process lines. As process resolution improves, masks can be shrunk by simply reducing λ, at least for λ greater than around $1\mu m$. However, as a consequence of the conservative nature of such rules, designs are not as economical in silicon area and may operate at reduced speed compared with circuits designed using μ rules. This is because the λ rules are a generalisation of μ rules and do not preserve many of the special cases which allow structures to be optimised.

2.2 Implementation schemes

2.2.1 Imposing geometric constraints

There are a number of schemes for implementing a design in an integrated circuit which are characterised by the degree of geometric patterning introduced, additional to the design rules. Such geometric constraints act at a higher level than the design rules and define in a broader sense the relationship between groups of devices and wiring areas. In this way a topological framework for the layout problem is formed. This is a useful method of reducing the complexity of the layout problem and accelerating the design and fabrication cycles. Knowledge of the additional constraints allows specialised techniques to exploit the topology. For example, a rectangular area with well defined points of wire entry and exit may be set aside for routing, and specific algorithms may be employed to solve this particular subclass of the layout problem.

A topological scheme may be fixed to such an extent that the number of masks which the designer is required to specify is reduced. This can lead to decreased manufacturing turnround time. However, these advantages come at the expense of silicon utilisation, since a rigid layout topology requires a high proportion of routing area to enable general circuits to be embedded. Further inefficiency may be introduced if elements of the design cannot be easily translated into the structures of the topological scheme, and must be constructed by some combination of features. Four schemes introducing geometric constraints are discussed below.

2.2.2 Custom

Layout in terms of design rules without any higher level constraints is known as custom design. This approach offers the greatest potential to fully utilise the available semiconductor area. In the extreme case the position of every component may be individually considered with the aim of optimising circuit performance or increasing density. The sizes of individual transistors may also be manipulated giving further opportunity for achieving efficiency. Such degrees of freedom in layout naturally attract overheads. The development time required to implement designs at this level of detail can be considerable, and as the size of the circuit increases this effect becomes more pronounced. The effort is only justified either by the long term savings in production costs, by the need for the very high performance achievable, or by the need to integrate the most complex circuit possible with a given yield.

Design automation of the greatest sophistication is important for custom design. By selectively choosing the level of detail at which to design, throughput is maximised and the design process becomes less error prone. The design automation system must manage the translation of data between different levels and should ensure conformance to design rules at all times. In practice a combination of techniques is employed. For example, at the lowest level transistors can be designed by hand, perhaps using an interactive graphics layout editor, and a macro cell might be created and stored in a library for future replication elsewhere. A special purpose logic synthesis program might be suitable for a complex boolean function which would be inefficiently constructed if combinations of standard logic gates were used, or the basic unit of a repetitive structure which might be hand optimised for a particular application. At a higher level, layout could be carried out in some symbolic notation, and at a higher level still, automated routing would be expected to act on areas defined by a mixture of automated and manual placement.

2.2.3 Standard cell

The standard cell approach introduces the notion of predefined logic and circuit elements. The electrical and geometrical properties of each cell are carefully designed. The cell can be generated at any point on the chip, subject to alignment with a grid which also defines the possible location of wiring. The cell library will usually be divided into a small number of classes of cells of the same height, and within each class the width of a cell is varied according to its complexity. Cells are placed in rows, creating rectangular wiring channels of varying size between pairs of rows. The cells are often designed such that power and a common signal such as a clock run through the cells along the rows. The cells vary in complexity and size from families of simple gates and flip-flops to more complex elements such as counters and memories. Specialised libraries may contain cells of even greater functionality, for example for processor or signal processing applications.

It is frequently appropriate to design with increasing levels of detail. At the least detailed level, blocks of logic can be allocated rectangular areas in which to be implemented. These physical blocks can be arranged to fit the chip area by floor planning. Blocks can be of a variety of shapes. For example, a memory block may be square, while the natural layout for a first-in first-out (FIFO) register may result in an elongated block. Each block has a physical interface which describes the location on the block boundary of the inter-block connections which must be made. This interface, and the physical dimensions of the block form the constraints for lower level layout of the internal details. Placement of cells within a block will aim to reduce connection lengths and channel widths. The assignment of cells to rows within the block can be guided by heuristic algorithms, often employing iterative improvement. Transformations of cells such as rotations and reflections are often catered for, giving the ability to change the orientation of cells within rows and of rows within blocks. Routing between cell rows is reduced to the channel routing problem, which is well understood, and algorithms exist for assigning nets to tracks in the channel while keeping channel density to a minimum. Global routing between blocks can be achieved by an area router.

2.2.4   Gate array

The gate array involves a level of severe geometric constraint. It is based on the concept of a regular array of logic sites and connection channels, which have passed through all stages of fabrication apart from the final interconnect metallisation. The manufacturer can therefore stockpile wafers, and the customer embeds the required circuit in the gate array by specifying the final set of metallisation masks. The nature of the logic site varies from array to array, and an array may have more than one type of logic site. For example, a site may be a single gate or a memory cell. A number of sites may be gathered in strips or blocks, and more complex cells such as flip-flops can be macro generated by specifying a pattern of interconnection to be imposed upon such a strip or block.

Since resist exposure and metal etching is a cheap process which does not require a full process capability, it can be done by a silicon broker. Furthermore, the regularity of the array constrains the layout problem such that fully automated placement and routing systems are self contained and relatively simple. However, this constraint also reduces gate utilisation, and the useful gate count of the array is typically 80% of the total gate count of perhaps ten thousand. The inflexible nature of the position and availability of routing may render it impossible to embed a circuit in the array, even if the gate count of the array appears to be large enough.

A class of gate array without explicit routing channels, in which the logic sites are adjacent is known as a 'sea of gates'. Wiring can be routed through sites where the site configuration permits. Alternatively sites can be allocated exclusively for routing purposes. Such arrays are usually dense, and can contain as many as one hundred thousand gates. However, utilisation is necessarily less than in arrays with explicit routing channels, perhaps 50%. 'Sea of gates' arrays require more sophisticated layout techniques, since the allocation of logic sites must be compact, but at the same time must leave sufficient space to complete the routing.

2.2.5   Field-programmable devices

Fully fabricated devices containing field-programmable structures represent the ultimate topological constraint. Such devices are more accurately a vehicle for circuit design rather than chip design. They are, however, emerging as an increasingly powerful method of hardware implementation as they become more complex. The simplest devices synthesise combinational logic functions by programming an AND-OR array where each output is formed from the OR of some intermediate product terms, each of which is the AND of some of the inputs. The number of functions is determined by the number of outputs while the number of inputs and intermediate terms determine the size of the chip and the complexity of the functions. Programming technology has developed from the one-shot blowing of fuses to the switching on or off of FETs by building or dissipating the charge on an electrically isolated gate. The latter form of programming is semi-permanent, being erasable by electrical or electromagnetic radiation means.

More complex and useful programmable devices allow sequential circuits to be built by incorporating sets of latches at the inputs and outputs and the feedback of output terms to the inputs. The connectivity of these features is programmable in a similar way to the AND-OR array. Yet more general systems have banks of components varying in complexity from I/O buffers, gates and flip-flops to shift registers, multiplexers and adders, surrounding a large switch matrix. At such scales, and with the potential for high volume mass-production and low cost, such programmable devices begin to obviate the need for application specific integration, especially when the devices are reusable.

2.2.6   Comparisons

A number of factors influencing the selection of an implementation scheme are outlined below. Some factors compromise each other and the final choice will result
from a tradeoff of one or more factors against the others.

Size. The level of integration required clearly affects the choice. The useful gate
count of the largest gate arrays is around 50,000. Larger designs are likely to include
more regular structures, which are inefficiently handled by gate array methods.
Standard cell techniques are better suited to larger circuits, especially where the cell
library is rich and includes many larger cells such as memory. The added flexibility
and sophistication of a custom layout scheme affords much greater utilisation. The
largest chip size which still enjoys a tolerable yield can be developed using custom
design.

Performance. High speed designs rely not only on the choice of technology and
logic family but on the quality of the layout. Reducing the average interconnect
length, resistance and capacitance reduces the signal propagation delay. In particular, if certain critical signals are preferentially assigned to short tracks there can
be an overall improvement in circuit performance. Very high performance therefore
requires custom methods to reduce interconnect lengths and control critical paths.
The density of standard cell design can approach that of custom design especially for
combinations of largely regular structures connected by data buses. Furthermore,
both custom and standard cell design can make use of appropriately chosen drivers
for signals on critical paths. The performance achievable in gate arrays is limited
by the invariant position and nature of the logic sites.

Cost. For very high production volumes a design needs to be as compact as possible.
This reduces the cost per unit by increasing the number of working chips per wafer.
An additional element of cost is the expense of design time and automation tools.
Custom design of large circuits can take many man years and involve significant
design automation support. These costs must be amortised by the savings achievable
for volume production. The simplicity of gate array design compensates for the
relatively high cost per chip, but only for modest volumes. Standard cell design
falls in a middle ground, with the potential for compact designs suitable for mass-
production, and with a high degree of efficient automation.

Turnround. Both custom and standard cell schemes require a full set of mask
and process steps, involving delays of weeks or even months. This is contrasted
by the turnround for gate array customisation which may be just a few days. In

the same fabrication process, the number of mask steps is typically fifteen and five respectively. An additional element of delay is the time required for testing of samples and implementation of design modifications, which may require a number of iterations before production begins. This delay is reduced for gate array designs where highly characterised cell behaviour and simply modelled wiring delays enable simulation delays to increase the chance of first time success. For standard cell and particularly custom schemes, the more random topology and greater variety of device types makes such simulation less representative, and prediction of design behaviour may be required at the transistor or circuit level, which can be costly and time consuming.

2.3 A descriptive framework

2.3.1 Hierarchies of abstraction

The importance of abstraction in design automation has already been mentioned. Another fundamental technique in the design process is the introduction of hierarchy. Hierarchy is a division into groups identified by some common property or properties with an order or ranking implied amongst the groups. Combining the two notions and defining hierarchies of abstraction forms a common paradigm for problem solving, particularly the problem of computer aided design of integrated circuits. The lowest level of abstraction corresponds to the design rules of the process. The highest level might be a description of the required functionality of the chip. An enforced hierarchic structure provides a framework for solving the design problem at progressively lower levels of abstraction, until the lowest level is reached.

Computer automation should manage the acquisition and manipulation of data at each level and ensure the consistency of data between levels. A goal of computer aided design is the automatic translation of data between different levels. Translation may be straightforward at lower levels, but becomes harder as the level of abstraction increases. Frequently, translations are applied in sequence so that data from a high level is translated via intermediate levels to a lower level. It is interesting to consider what the minimum volume of user data required to produce the intended circuit would be, and what form this input would take. This volume of input probably relates to the sophistication of the abstractions at the highest level for which there is a series of automatic translations which reach the lowest level.

2.3.2   A framework

A framework for describing the abstractions of the design automation problem is shown in Figure 2.2. The framework introduces two types of hierarchy. The first type defines three problem domains relating to behavioural, structural and phys-ical properties. The behavioural domain describes the functionality of the circuit. This involves a description of the action of the circuit outputs in response to se-quences of circuit inputs. The abstractions in the behavioural domain exclude any notions of structure or implementation. The structural domain introduces compo-nents and modules, or groups of components, and describes how they are connected to achieve a designated behaviour. This involves a logical specification of the con-nections between modules and components. Details of technology and module or component layout are excluded. The physical domain describes how the components and connections of the structural level are positioned and implemented in a partic-ular technology. The second class of hierarchy divides each problem domain into levels of symbolic abstraction. Within each problem domain, the level of symbolism decreases from top to bottom. The higher the level of symbolism the more concise the description.

The framework can be used to classify design automation tools in terms of the level at which they manipulate data, or in terms of the levels between which they translate data. The design process can be viewed as threading through the framework using manipulation and translation tools. In the framework, the level decreases as the design moves down and to the right. The aim is therefore to enter data in the behavioural domain, which is automatically translated to data at the physical mask level. This is a very difficult problem, since all the intervening structural and physical levels must be synthesised from purely behavioural descriptions. In general, this has not yet been achieved, and design is more likely to be somewhere in the structural domain. Brief descriptions of the key types of manipulation and translation tools are given below. A more detailed introduction with reference to specific design automation tools is given in [Weste 85].

2.3.3   Manipulation

Tools for the input and editing of notation are required for any level in the framework at which the designer wishes to work. This might perhaps be done textually using a syntax directed editor to input statements in a structural hardware description language (HDL) [Lattice 82], or graphical input might include the use of layout

Problem domain

Behavioural	Structural	Physical
Sequential	*Module*	*Block*
• Description of output behaviour as a function of inputs and time.	• Hierarchic description of connectivity in terms of 'black box' nodes of arbitrary complexity.	• Hierarchic description of physical geometry of modules.
• Descriptions often tailored to specific target architectures such as:	• Nodes have defined interfaces and are connected by signals.	• Sizes and positions of nodes, interfaces and signals.
– Processor design,	• Nodes have implicit, assumed behaviour.	• **Notation:** Tile and corner-stitching.
– Register transfer.	• **Notation:** Hierarchic hardware description language, register transfer functions.	*Stick*
• Alternatively descriptions in terms of algorithms for which hardware modules are known such as:		• Stylised description of circuit topology.
	Gate	• Relative positions of transistors and wiring.
– Signal processing,	• Description of connectivity in terms of simple nodes.	• **Notation:** Line drawings, virtual grid.
– Parallel data flow.	• Boolean logic gates, flip-flops and simple functions.	
• **Notation:** Behavioural description languages, high-level languages, finite state machines.	• **Notation:** Simple flat hardware description language.	*Symbolic*
Combinational		• Description of actual location of transistors and wiring.
• Description of output behaviour solely as a function of inputs.	*Circuit*	• Symbolic masks for diffusion, polysilicon and metallisation.
• Typical target architecture is the programmable logic array.	• Description of connectivity in terms of primitive nodes.	• **Notation:** Colour-coded overlapping rectangles.
• **Notation:** Boolean logic.	• Transistors, capacitors and resistors.	*Mask*
	• **Notation:** Node and netlist.	• Description of actual location of all features.
		• Full set of mask details.
		• **Notation:** Polygon geometry.

Figure 2.2: A framework of design automation abstractions

editors to manipulate shapes at the physical level [Fairbairn 78]. After input, the
first operation is to interpret or compile the descriptions into a database which
supports the management and exchange of data formats between levels. This might
be a netlist of nodes and signals or a hierarchical decomposition into polygons.

Simulation of the circuit is a key tool in the structural domain. By assigning behavioural models to nodes and connections in the structure, the response of the
circuit to external stimuli can be predicted. These models are not derived from
descriptions in the behavioural domain, but are parameterised by device properties
of the structural or physical domains. For gate level simulation, the models are
based on the laws of boolean logic and simple delay calculations [Newton 80]. For
circuit level simulation, the models are based on electrical behaviour and can involve lengthy calculation [Nage 75]. The purpose of simulation is to compare the
predicted behaviour with the required behaviour.

Another important area is testing. Fabricated chips are tested by stimulating circuit inputs with test patterns and matching actual against expected output patterns.
The testability of a design is a measure of how simply and thoroughly the chips can
be tested. Testability is a static property of the structure which can be quantified by
analysis [Goldstein 79]. Test patterns can be automatically generated, and the effectiveness of a set of patterns at determining the presence of a fault can be evaluated
by fault simulation which predicts the circuit behaviour in the presence of faults
of some specific nature, such as stuck-at-0 and stuck-at-1 faults [Bruer 77]. Design
for increased testability includes the addition of a testing mode and additional logic
either to shift internal values in and out [Eichelberger 77], or self testing by gener-
ating pseudo random binary sequences which cause an output signature which can
be analysed [El Ziq 83].

In the behavioural domain there are operations such as function minimisation at
the combinational level [Gunrath 89]. Carefully chosen notation allows automated
deduction and reasoning to be used. For example, if the structural specification
and required behaviour are couched in the language of formal logic, then theorem
provers can be used to verify the correctness of the specification [Stavridou 88].

2.3.4   Translation

Ideally, translation should be necessary only in the direction from behavioural to
physical mask levels. This necessitates correct translation, and should forbid manual
intervention in any automatically generated lower level. Such intervention introduces

the possibility of violating higher level intentions. It is still common, however, to permit such editing. As a result, translations in the reverse direction are provided to generate higher level descriptions which can, with difficulty, be compared with the original. The classic example is the process of circuit extraction, which recreates a description at the structural circuit level from the physical mask level [Hofmann 83]. Netlist comparison attempts to match the original and recreated structural descriptions, an added problem usually being the lack of full net names in the recreated description [Spickelmier 83].

For the structural and physical domains, translation in the forward direction is performed by layout. This topic is a cornerstone of automated design and is usually divided into placement and routing phases. This division simplifies both placement and routing algorithms, though the phases are dependent in that placement defines both the space for the routing and the location of the interfaces which must visited by a signal. As an example of placement, floor planning translates descriptions at the structural module level to the physical block level by assigning and positioning rectangles and interface locations [Ying 89]. Routing space is implicitly created in the channels between rectangles. At a lower module and block level, placement might consist of the assignment of gates to positions within cell rows or at sites on a gate array [Dunlop 85]. The three-dimensional implementations of these techniques are discussed in chapter four.

Routing is an embedding of the structural connectivity into a physical grid. Placement reserves areas for routing, and determines the positions of the interfaces at the block, cell or transistor level. Specialised routers exist for geometrically constrained situations such as the rectangular channel between two rows of cells in a block [Burstein 83]. Less efficient but more general purpose routers are suitable for the connections between blocks. Many are derived from an early maze router [Lee 61]. Translation between a stick level virtual grid description and the lowest physical levels involves the translation of the virtual grid into a real one, the generation of transistors and wiring and the physical compaction of the resulting layout [Dunlop 80].

Translation from the behavioural domain to physical mask level is often referred to as silicon compilation. This involves the synthesis of structure from functionality. This is well understood for combinational logic [Newton 85], but not for sequential systems for which there are no completely general mechanisms. Early systems were characterised by the notion of a target floor plan with a fixed number of rows of cells and offered limited design space exploration, often with a fixed architecture in mind such as microprocessor design [Johannsen 78] or signal processing [Denyer 82].

More general methods include the use of expert systems drawing on a large knowledge base of circuit structures each with functional descriptions from which larger designs can be built [Kowalsky 83]. For example, a system can contain the structure corresponding to rules describing inversion, delay and counting.

Another similar method is to design by combining parameterised behavioural models for which it is known how to generate layout [Buric 83]. When structure is derived from a model, the parameters to the model may control the size of the structure, or modify its behaviour in some known way. For example, the behavioural model for a shift register might have a parameter giving the length of the register. The model for a general finite state machine might have parameter arrays of arbitrary size describing input stimuli and output response. The structure for this can be automatically generated by standard methods of finite state machine synthesis. Overall behaviour can be verified by simulation before synthesis takes place.

The analysis of dataflow in high-level language models has been used recently in the synthesis of register transfer functions at the structural level [Camposano 89]. Register transfer functions describe the structure of a system in terms of registers each latched at one of two clock phases with blocks of combinational logic interspersed between the blocks. Such functions can be automatically translated from the structural to the physical domains.

2.4   Case study

2.4.1   A network controller

An example of the design and implementation of a network control system is now presented. The Cambridge Fast Ring (CFR) [Hopper 88] was based on experiences with the earlier Cambridge Ring, a communication system based on the empty slot principle. Both rings were devised in the Cambridge University Computer Laboratory. The goal was to design a faster communication medium for applications at the local and metropolitan area network level. An important requirement was the integration of the control system to reduce cost and improve reliability.

The integration of the CFR is an interesting example as it was first attempted using gate array technology and finally completed using standard cell methods. Therefore the relative merits of the two approaches can be compared and contrasted. The design has structures found in many digital circuits such as registers, memory elements, data buses and random logic. The design automation tools for both implementations were purpose built in order to provide effective and adaptable simulation and layout tools.

2.4.2 Gate array implementation

A high speed network requires high performance hardware. Ideally, the design would be implemented in a single high performance custom chip. However, the low projected production volumes did not justify the financial cost. A compromise was found with high-speed bipolar gate arrays manufactured by Texas Instruments. These offered speed by virtue of very fast logic, and simplicity of implementation by virtue of the gate array technique. The initial system design was at the top structural level, and involved four components. These were two application specific integrated circuits (ASIC) containing primarily random logic and registers, a 64Kbit DRAM to hold an address map, and data buffering. Of the ASICs, a smaller one of around 600 gates was to control the address logic of the map and associated functions, while a larger one of some 1800 gates contained the primary network control logic. The arrays were based on very fast wire-OR logic with gate delays of around 5ns. The basic site was fixed, a four input NAND gate. Groups of around ten gates were interspersed by a regular grid of interconnect. This took the form of two layers of metallisation, an advanced process in 1982.

A number of problems were encountered, falling into three categories. First, problems occur with fixed site arrays in general. Consider the four input NAND site. An inverter can be created by tying three of the inputs to logic level one, but the cell has four times the number of transistors necessary. Also, a five input NAND can be synthesised with three gates (Figure 2.3(a)). A second problem involved a combination of the design and technology features. The design required certain groups of signals to have balanced delays. The technology provided very fast gates, but relatively slow wiring which therefore dominated the total delay. Balancing required careful matching of track lengths and delay chains, which coupled with an asymmetry of rise and fall times complicated the placement and routing process. Third, the logic had a limited drive capability, and the fan-out for a gate was severely constrained. This problem was solved by building fan-out trees (Figure 2.3(b)), but the layout problem was compounded where such trees formed part of a balanced net.

After the initial system level design, detailed structural design at the gate level was done. This was carried out manually in pictorial form. The netlist implied

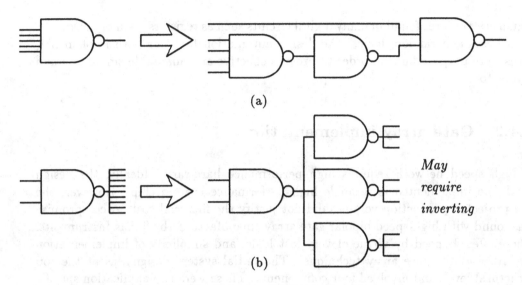

(a)

(b)

Figure 2.3: Inefficiencies of fixed site gate arrays

by the drawings was then coded into the design automation system. The basis of this system was an experimental design automation project [Robinson 82] which provided the netlist entry and basic simulator mechanisms. One interesting feature was the description of the netlist in the language in which the system was written, Algol68, enabling concise procedural descriptions to be made.

Event driven gate level simulation was used to verify the design and to match delays. The signal changes predicted at the output pins were checked informally by visual inspection against the expected behaviour. The success of this method of structural verification relies on the formulation of 'good' sequences of stimuli at the input pins. A set of 'good' sequences would be expected to simulate much of the correct behaviour of the circuit at least. Behaviour under incorrect input assertions was also investigated to some degree. Initially, a simple fixed delay model was used. This was replaced by a more sophisticated scheme with separate rise and fall delays for the gate output, and with different delays for different fan-out and fan-in loadings. In general, the models predicted circuit behaviour more accurately than the manufacturer's system of simulation.

Initially automatic layout was carried out using the manufacturer's software. The placement phase was entirely constructive, determined by cost function. An ink-blot type area router was deemed likely to succeed provided the estimated channel densities of the placement were within certain limits. However the gate count of the design approached the useful gate count of the array, around 1800 out of 2200, and a satisfactory placement satisfying the channel density criteria was not found. It was felt that the design would fit the array, and so rather than modify the design, placement improvement algorithms were developed.

Placement improvement was sought by iterative interchange. Two rectangles, possibly overlapping, delimited the source and destination ranges of the exchange of two randomly chosen gates. An improvement, or at least no degradation, in cost confirmed the swap. Gate positions could be fixed where the delay between gates was deemed critical, for example for matched delays and clock lines. The process was repeated many times using different sequences of random numbers, some solutions being better than others. The variance in results is usual in this type of iterative improvement and is because the simple strategy of pairwise interchange and evaluation of cost function is not able to distinguish between local and global cost minimisation. The interchange process was carried out in parallel on a number of processors connected to the Cambridge Distributed System [Needham 82], each processor exploring the solution obtained using a different random sequence. It was considered to include a periodic voting phase, whereby the most promising placements were redistributed amongst the participating processors. This was never fully implemented.

A placement satisfying the manufacturer's routing criteria was eventually found, and full routing was achieved. Unfortunately, these efforts were in vain, as the fabrication process and in particular the customisation proved unreliable. This was largely due to the use of two metal layers. The technological problems were not overcome, and the manufacturer withdrew the product.

2.4.3   Standard cell implementation

Following the abrupt end of the gate array implementation, the architecture for the network control system was revised. With increasingly easy access to VLSI manufacture, a greater degree of integration seemed possible. A small very fast chip to drive and receive the ring signal was designed to provide a byte wide interface to a larger network controller chip, with a 64Kbit DRAM to hold an address map as before. The small chip was implemented as a 400 gate ECL gate array. The network controller was byte oriented and so required clocking at only one eighth of the ECL clock speed. The target ring speed was 100Mbits/s and so the controller required a clock speed of only 12.5MHz. This was within the capabilities of CMOS logic. Since the controller design included FIFO buffers, standard cell implementation was a more natural choice than gate array with specially designed FIFO cells augmenting a cell library. Custom design was excluded for the same reasons as before.

The previous poor experiences with manufacturer's design automation software, and the encouraging experiences with purpose built tools suggested that it was sensible to implement a design automation system for standard cells. At the time, the simulation and layout tools which could be developed and used in the Computer Laboratory were more sophisticated than the tools available at the manufacturer's design centre. The initial goal was to provide simulation for both chips and layout of the standard cell chip. A complete redesign of the automation system accompanied the redesign of the network control system. The design automation project which had formed the basis of the gate array simulator had been rewritten in Modula2, and once again this was adopted as the basis of the automation system.

A feature of the new system was a hierarchical representation of structure and behaviour. Though elegant, the high-level language specification of the earlier system had drawbacks. In particular, since the structural description was represented statically by compiled code, circuit changes required a compilation of the module defining the structure, and the relinking of *all* the tools in the design automation suite. Another reason for abandoning this method of description was the need for a permanent updatable representation of the physical details. For simplicity, such details should be integrated with the structural representation. For this purpose, a simple hardware description language was developed allowing hierarchical descriptions at the structural and physical levels to be simply interpreted rather than compiled.

Once again, simulation was event driven with behaviour at any level in the structural hierarchy being specified by a procedure generic to that specific class of structure. In general, modelling was more sophisticated than for the previous system. Simulation was performed at two levels. Practical verification of the structure and detailed timing analysis was done by simulation with models at the cell level. The range of cells was large, including families of simple gates and flip-flops. Where possible, a single model was designed to work for a whole family of cells, for example all NAND gates were modelled by the same procedure. Models for flip-flops were considerably more complex, with large amounts of internal state required for good modelling.

Manufacturer's data was used to calculate the delays between the input and output pins of a cell as a function of the total capacitive load of the output and the direction of the logic change. A number of checks on circuit operation were automatically made. For example, the skew between low to high and high to low delays was constrained to lie within certain bounds, and the set-up and hold times for flip-flops were checked. The event scheduling mechanism was extended to handle tri-state and bidirectional buses, and violation of bus contention rules was automatically checked. Partly charged loads and the corresponding shrinking of pulses was accurately modelled, a useful enhancement avoiding misleading results which can occur with fixed delay calculation.

A much higher behavioural-level simulation was also undertaken. A complex model of the whole chip as a function of the input and output pins was written. Using the same simulation program, this model could be replicated to simulate the behaviour of several chips connected together. Furthermore, the ECL and DRAM chips were modelled, allowing high-level simulation of the complete system. In addition, a ring connecting both behavioural and structural models was simulated, serving as an informal check on the correspondence between the structural and behavioural specifications.

The physical framework for the layout phase was an $11\mu m$ grid. As usual with standard cell methods, cells were of fixed height and variable width, according to cell complexity. Cell dimensions were integer multiples of the grid size. Subject to simple rules for the positions and orientations of metal and polysilicon tracks and of vias between the two, rows and channels could be formed anywhere on the grid. The structural description described modules which were manipulated as a floor plan at the physical block level using a hierarchical layout editor. Each high-level block formed a domain for the automatic placement and routing of the logic contained. The required shape for the block determined the number of cell rows and wiring channels, and the relative positions of blocks in the floor plan could be used to indicate the approximate location of ports where global signals could cross block boundaries.

The placement had two phases. First, an assignment of cells to rows. Connected cells in non-adjacent rows require additional feedthrough cells in intervening rows. By aiming to minimise the number of feedthroughs required, both the interconnect length and area were reduced. An initial placement of half the nodes was made. Then, an iterative interchange phase completed the placement within each block. The interchange involved a cycle of swapping a pair of randomly chosen cells which reduced the cost, followed by the placement of some of the remaining cells. This process was repeated until all cells were placed. The advantage of such a process was that initially cells could migrate large distances with the likelihood of producing a better seed placement for the rest of the process. With the block fully placed, feedthrough cells were inserted in the relevant rows. This lead to an imbalance in row lengths, the inner rows typically containing more feedthroughs. A further swapping between rows was designed to improved the shape of the block.

The second placement phase improved the horizontal placement by random swapping within each row. The cost function here was an estimate of horizontal wire length, and the quality of the horizontal placement achieved directly affected the efficiency and density of the channel routing. The underlying strategy of the placement phase was to develop quick and simple improvements based on iterative interchange, which could be easily evaluated and then pursued or discarded. Cost functions were deliberately kept simple and free from detailed routing considerations.

The channel routing for each block was accomplished using a 'greedy routing algorithm' [Rivest 82]. Assignment of nets to channels is made for a whole column at once working from left to right. Where there exists an element of choice, a net is assigned temporarily to more than one channel. When the net reaches the destination, or the channel becomes congested, a particular channel assignment for the net is chosen from the alternatives, releasing the remainder. Routing between the ends of the channels and the ports on the block boundary was accomplished using channels orthogonal to the rows. Global routing between floor plan blocks was done manually with the aid of the layout editor. Throughout the routing phase certain signals, such as the system clock, were preferentially assigned to metal tracks thereby helping to ensure lower wiring delays for those signals.

An important phase of the design verification was a re-simulation of the circuit using capacitance values extracted from the dimensions of the proposed layout. An optimistic model of track delay is to view the resistance and capacitance of the track to be lumped together. A pessimistic model of track delay is to view the resistance and capacitance as separate. Logic level simulation was carried out using both models with the hope that correct simulation output at the two extremes would imply correct behaviour for more typical but harder to model cases. Certain key structures such as bidirectional buses and associated control logic were further checked with a proprietary circuit level simulator, where the delay model is a distributed resistor capacitor network.

The chip was successfully manufactured in 3μm technology. The layout of the CFR is used in chapter eight in comparison with three-dimensional layouts of the same circuit.

Chapter 3

Three-Dimensional Chip Technology

3.1 Isolation techniques

3.1.1 Introduction

In conventional two-dimensional integrated circuits, transistor channels are isolated from each other by the bulk resistivity of the substrate. Transistor gate and wiring levels are isolated from the channels and from each other by layers of grown insulator, such as silicon dioxide. Three-dimensional circuits require similar isolation between planes of devices in addition to that within each plane. Isolation techniques, originally developed to enhance two-dimensional device characteristics, provide the base technology for three-dimensional circuit structures. Isolated structures are characterised by a thin semiconducting layer above an insulating layer, and for silicon based technology the term silicon on insulator (SOI) is widely used. The semiconductor layer is patterned and etched using conventional techniques, leaving islands where devices are to be constructed. Useful properties of isolated circuits include:

- Low junction capacitances and correspondingly fast circuits, by extending the channel regions to the insulating layer (Figure 3.1(a)),

- Latch-up (Figure 3.1(b)) virtually eliminated in CMOS circuits, since there are fewer opportunities for parasitic junctions to be formed,

- Denser structures due to the absence of bulky wells and further performance gains due to the correspondingly shorter wiring runs,

- Enhanced alpha-particle radiation tolerance due to smaller junction areas.

A number of isolation techniques are described below with particular reference to three-dimensional structures.

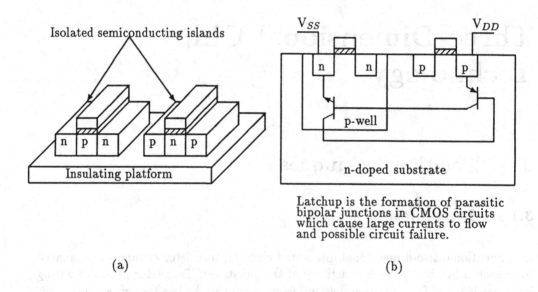

Latchup is the formation of parasitic bipolar junctions in CMOS circuits which cause large currents to flow and possible circuit failure.

(a)   (b)

Figure 3.1: Isolated circuits

3.1.2 Epitaxy

The earliest SOI structures involved the growth of a thin epitaxial layer of single crystal silicon on a sapphire substrate [Manasevit 64]. Sapphire has a similar crystalline structure to silicon, thereby seeding the growth process. However, very low yields have confined such technology to applications requiring high performance and a high degree of radiation tolerance. Such applications are often military. More recently, a technique is described where a thin silicon film is grown by solid phase epitaxy over an epitaxially grown calcium fluoride insulating layer [Onoda 87]. The formation of a number of epitaxially grown layers is known as heteroepitaxy. The interest in gallium arsenide semiconductors extends to the fabrication of isolated structures, and an analogous technique for the construction of FETs in a thin gallium arsenide film deposited by molecular beam epitaxy is reported in [Tsutsui 87].

An alternative technique is to open seeding windows in an insulating structure, providing contact to a single crystal substrate (Figure 3.2). Solid phase epitaxy of deposited amorphous silicon begins in the seeding window, and then spreads laterally over the insulating patterns [Hirashita 89]. The insulating patterns may be any oxide capped device [Friedrich 89], and the overgrowth of high quality single crystal silicon has clear possibilities for three-dimensional integration.

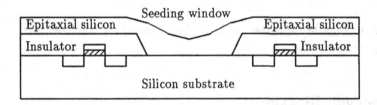

Figure 3.2: Seeded lateral epitaxy

3.1.3   Wafer bonding

A mechanical method of creating SOI structures is to bond two wafer structures together [Lasky 86]. This is achieved by pressing together the naturally oxidised surfaces of the two wafers and then inserting the combination into a hot oxidising atmosphere. The wafers are forced into intimate contact by atmospheric pressure on their outer surface when a partial vacuum is formed in the gap between the two. The vacuum is due to the conversion of the intervening gaseous oxygen into silicon dioxide when a chemical bond is formed between the wafers. The two wafers are referred to as the handle and seed wafers (Figure 3.3).

It is claimed that the handle wafer can be any structure capped with a planar oxide layer. The seed wafer forms the SOI layer, and is constructed from a conventional wafer with a thin epitaxially grown silicon layer capped with insulator. After bonding, the seed wafer is etched back to the epitaxial layer. The exposed silicon on insulator surface can then be processed by standard techniques. The attractive properties for three-dimensional structures are thin insulator layers suitable

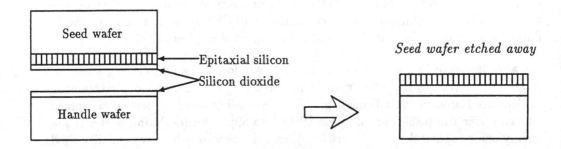

Figure 3.3: Wafer bonding

for gate oxide, negligible capacitance at the bond interface, and low temperature of the bonding process.

3.1.4   Recrystallisation

One of the most researched methods of forming insulated structures is the recrystallisation of thin polycrystalline films deposited on an insulating layer. A conventional silicon wafer usually forms a uniform platform for the growth of the insulator which is typically a layer of silicon-dioxide between 0.5 and 1.0μm thick. A polysilicon film of similar thickness is grown by chemical vapour deposition (CVD) and finally a capping layer of insulator is deposited. The composite is heated and the polysilicon melts. On cooling a single crystal silicon layer forms which can be processed with conventional techniques. The crystal structure of the recrystallised layer may be mixed. As for epitaxially grown layers, more precisely oriented crystal structures can be achieved by opening seeding windows in the insulating layer.

A number of heating techniques have been successfully employed. The composite is usually held at a raised temperature by back heating. Many experiments use a scanning laser beam to cause local melting, and an early example of an SOI MOSFET fabricated in a laser melted film is described in [Lee 79]. CMOS transistors have been fabricated in films melted by graphite strip heaters [Tsaur 82]. Other methods of heating include the use of electron beams [Hopper 84] and an incoherent light source [Electronics 85a].

More recently bipolar transistors have been fabricated in thin recrystallised films [Sturm 85], [Colinge 86]. BiCMOS circuits are particularly suited to SOI technology [Tsaur 84], since the complete device isolation offered simplifies integration and results in greater packing density than the other methods previously described for the co-integration of bipolar and CMOS transistors. Recrystallisation can be successful on transparent quartz substrates. This has applications in display technology. High voltage thin film MOSFETs can be arranged in a matrix to address electroluminescent displays [Unagami 88].

The electrical properties of recrystallised films compare favourably with conventional silicon substrate technology. Seeded processes produce films with electron mobility equal to that found in bulk silicon, while unseeded processes have lower electron mobilities. Both seeded and unseeded transistors have hole mobilities close to that of bulk silicon transistors. Latch-up in CMOS circuits is eliminated by complete device isolation, stray capacitances are low and circuit densities are high. Recrystallised SOI is an ideal medium for VLSI, and as one of the more mature isolation techniques has been the technological base of many of the three-dimensional integrated structures described below.

3.2   Three-dimensional structures

3.2.1   Hybrid structures

The use of three dimensions is not new in the history of electronics. Hybrid three-dimensional circuits have employed each new development in electronics, from valves to transistors to integrated circuits. A very early example dating from 1951 is Project Tinkertoy [Dukes 61]. This was a stack of small (2cm×2cm) ceramic or glass hybrid integrated circuits connected at the edges by vertical metal wiring. Each layer contained passive components such as resistors, capacitors and inductors. The active component, a thermionic valve, was connected by a valve socket mounted on the upper surface of the top layer. Several modules were connected on a printed circuit board. The layers were selected, stacked and mechanically and electrically joined by automatic assembly machines.

A similar structure dating from 1958 was the Micromodule [Dukes 61] which was an order of magnitude smaller yet functionally more complex. The single valve was replaced by one or more layers each containing a single transistor. A very dense three-dimensional cellular processor architecture has been developed by Hughes Research Laboratories [Grinberg 84]. A novel connection method provides vertical wiring between stacks of wafers (Figure 3.4).

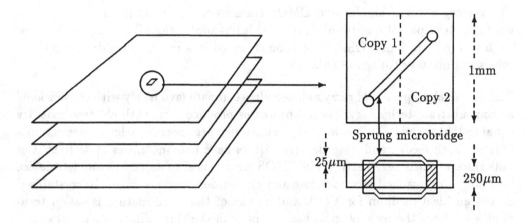

Figure 3.4: A three-dimensional wafer stack

Each wafer contains a 32 × 32 array of identical processing elements such as accumulators or registers. An array of processors is built by stacking wafers containing the different elements. Each cell has a single connection to the adjacent wafers, forming a vertical bus. A wafer providing program storage and sequencing controls the flow of data between the elements on the different wafers in the manner of a conventional von Neumann machine. Redundancy at the cell level is provided by a duplicate circuit and discretionary disconnection of either circuit. The vertical connection is provided by means of a sprung microbridge, which compensates for wafer warping.

3.2.2 Multi-layer wiring

Typical fabrication processes allow for one layer of polysilicon and one or two layers of metal wiring. This is a minimum requirement for the efficient routing of large circuits. As mentioned earlier, the polysilicon layer can be made less resistive by combining it with a refractory metal to form a silicide. The gate material can therefore be used for longer distances of wiring. More complex processes allow for three or more layers of metallisation [Moriya 83]. Such multi-layer structures are sometimes described as 'two-and-a-half-dimensional'.

As the number of layers of wiring and therefore the number of processing steps increases, the yield suffers and the cost increases. This can in part be justified by the benefits of producing more compact circuit layouts due to the availability of wiring and the ease of placement and routing. However, there is a useful limit on the number of wiring levels, beyond which there is little benefit. It has been shown that for certain classes of routing problem, in particular a restricted class of channel routing problems, three layers are sufficient [Preparata 82]. Another theory suggests a useful limit on the number of layers for more general circuits, and is part of a larger work on three-dimensional layouts [Leighton 83]. This is the subject of further discussion in the next chapter.

3.2.3 Monolithic structures

For the full potential of three-dimensional structures to be realised, transistors must be distributed in three dimensions by fabrication rather than packaging techniques. This is the only way to achieve high vertical density, more than an order of magnitude greater than that demonstrated by Hughes. Some examples of three-dimensional circuits which have been fabricated are presented below. These circuits fall into two groups, homogeneous circuits where the same logic family is used throughout the layers, and heterogeneous circuits where devices from different logic families are combined.

One of the first three-dimensional circuits is reported in [Gibbons 80]. The homogeneous structure is a two transistor inverter with a common gate between the two layers (Figure 3.5(a)). A p-type transistor is fabricated in conventional n-type bulk silicon up to and including the construction of the polysilicon gate. Then an insulating layer, which will be the gate oxide of the upper n-type transistor is deposited, followed by a polysilicon layer. This is laser recrystallised and the n-type transistor is built in the recrystallised film. The device has good characteristics, and clearly offers circuits an immediate saving in bulk silicon area. The use of a common joined gate has been termed JMOS by some.

The first example of completely isolated vertically stacked transistors with independent gates is reported in [Kawamura 83]. A p-type transistor is created in an n-doped substrate (Figure 3.5(b)). A layer of phosphor silicate glass provides the necessary insulating layer. The second layer of transistors is then fabricated using an unseeded laser recrystallisation process, which has been shown not to degrade the electrical characteristics of the underlying bulk transistors [Kawamura 84b]. Connection between top and bottom layers is achieved by the etching of contact holes

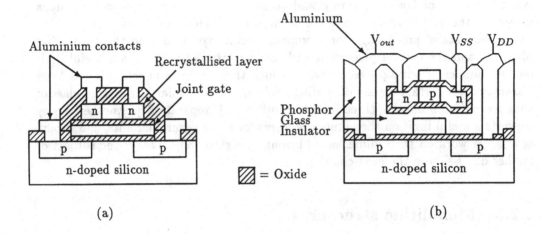

Figure 3.5: Three-dimensional structures

followed by aluminium metallisation.

The next development was a structure with two layers of transistors each constructed in recrystallised films [Kawamura 84a]. In an attempt to demonstrate the
feasibility and potential benefits of three-dimensional integration, a gate array composed of two input NAND cells containing vertically stacked transistors was fabricated. The layout of a conventional two input NAND gate was folded into two
layers each with two transistors. The characteristics of the cell were shown to be
good, and the creation of test circuits with properties comparable to equivalent
two-dimensional circuits demonstrated the viability of using multiple recrystallised
layers for integrated circuit fabrication. Three stacked layers of transistors are reported in [Sugahara 86]. In this structure NMOS transistors were created in the
bulk silicon substrate and in each of two recrystallised layers. Connection in the
lower two levels was by the polysilicon gate layer in order to withstand the high
temperature recrystallisation process.

The heteroepitaxial isolation technique has also been applied to three-dimensional
integration [Sugiura 85]. Epitaxial layers of silicon were grown on insulating layers
of epitaxially grown boron phosphide. Up to four pairs of layers were grown, and
the characteristics of transistors fabricated in each layer were determined, showing
some degradation in the upper layers. An advantage of this technique for three-
dimensional circuits is that the boron phosphide can be made conductive by implantation. This could be used to provide connections between adjacent silicon

layers.

A three-dimensional BiCMOS structure is reported in [Geis 86]. Bipolar power transistors are created in the substrate, and NMOS transistors in an upper recrystallised layer. This is an example of a class of circuits to have attracted some interest. Elements of circuitry requiring different technologies can be fabricated in different layers, and the integration of complete systems is possible. For example, a four-layer structure as shown in Figure 3.6 could be fabricated. The top layer might contain analogue sensing elements while middle layers could contain analogue-to-digital conversion circuitry and signal processing logic. The lowest level could contain power transistors with drive capability. Systems with optical elements, either light emitting for display purposes [Unagami 88], or light sensing for camera purposes [Fujii 88] have been considered.

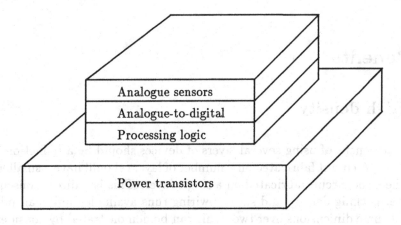

Figure 3.6: A multi-function three-dimensional structure

3.2.4   Memory applications

Some of the most obvious applications for three-dimensional integration are memory circuits. Highly regular design and a clear division of functionality makes memory a strong candidate for the first commercially available three-dimensional circuits. A 256 bit SRAM fabricated in two transistor layers is reported in [Inou 86]. A total of some 1500 NMOS transistors are used in the construction of six-transistor memory cells in the silicon substrate. The address decoding, sense amplifier and

I/O buffering circuits are constructed using some 600 CMOS transistors in a stacked recrystallised layer. Around 100 inter-layer connections are made, over half of which carry the power supply to the lower layer. A much larger three-dimensional static RAM organised into 8K × 8 bits contains over 400,000 transistors [Hite 85]. Both memories have an access time of around 100ns.

DRAM circuits have also been integrated using three-dimensional structures. The conventional two-dimensional one transistor cell has a switching transistor adjacent to a trench capacitor. By fabricating the transistor in a recrystallised polysilicon layer, the capacitor can be folded underneath the transistor thereby reducing the base area of the cell by roughly a factor of two [Sturm 84]. A stacked two transistor cell with adjacent capacitor is reported to achieve a high level of alpha-particle radiation immunity while occupying the same area as a conventional one transistor cell [Terada 87].

3.3 Benefits

3.3.1 High density

An immediate benefit of using several layers of devices should be a reduction in the total area used. A circuit fabricated on a number of layers should have a smaller total area than the same circuit fabricated on a single layer. This is a direct consequence of the greater packing density and shorter wiring runs available, and is an inherent advantage of three dimensions over two. This can be demonstrated by considering a simple half-adder circuit embedded in both two- and three-dimensional rectangular grids (Figure 3.7). In the grids, nodes can correspond to the gates of the circuit and edges correspond to connecting wires. In the two-dimensional layout (Figure 3.7(b)), five additional nodes W must be introduced in order to provide the necessary edges to complete the circuit connections. In the three-dimensional layout (Figure 3.7(c)), the gates of the circuit can be assigned to the nodes of the grid such that all the circuit connections are completed by virtue of the relative positions of the gates alone. This simple example indicates the increased opportunities for placement and routing in three-dimensional grids.

Greater density will also be achieved in circuits with several layers by reducing the number of bulky I/O buffers required. For example, a four layer three-dimensional circuit where each layer provides the functionality of a two-dimensional integrated circuit needs only one set of I/O buffers. The reduction in the number of buffers may attract an even greater saving in power consumption. This is important in reducing the heat which must be dissipated.

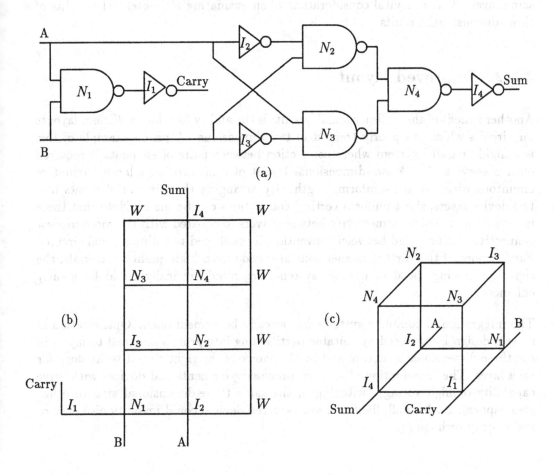

Figure 3.7: Layout of a half-adder circuit in two- and three-dimensional grids

The simple grids of Figure 3.7 depict unit dimensions in all directions. In practice there is a most important reduction in the vertical separation between transistors on adjacent layers. Within each layer, the separation of transistors is the same as would be found in a two-dimensional isolation process. For example, using λ based design rules for SOI, the minimum separation between gates of p-type and n-type transistors in an inverter is about 10λ. However, the vertical separation of two such transistors in a two layer layout is simply the combined thickness of the insulating and recrystallised layers. This is typically λ. The separation between transistors in adjacent layers is potentially much smaller than that between transistors in the same layer. This is a vital consideration when evaluating the potential benefits of three-dimensional circuits.

3.3.2   Improved layout

Another benefit of three-dimensional circuits is the ability to achieve efficient layouts for circuits which are poorly treated in two dimensions. A prime example of this is a highly parallel system where connection between pairs of elements is required on a massive scale. A two-dimensional layout of this involves a large amount of circuitous wiring of non-uniform length. By arranging the pairs of elements into two device layers, short uniform vertical connections can be made. Note that there is potentially massive connectivity between layers, compared with the more modest connectivity to be found between conventionally packaged two-dimensional circuits. Furthermore, if the vertical connections are made from high quality materials, the signal processing speed of parallel systems organised vertically could be greatly enhanced.

The integration of complete systems has already been mentioned. Optimisation of system design is enhanced by suitable partitioning into groups assigned to layers in the three-dimensional structure and by the choice of the right circuit technology for each layer. The combination of sensors, processing elements and devices with drive capability or high voltage switching in the same three-dimensional structure has great appeal. Such small, light and low powered devices could revolutionise camera and display technology.

3.3.3   High speed

A number of factors indicate that three-dimensional circuits can exhibit high performance. First, the greater density mentioned above reduces interconnect length and propagation delay. Second, the integration of several functions avoids the use of I/O buffers and long off-chip connections. Third, the isolation techniques employed in the fabrication of three-dimensional circuits produce small thin-film transistors on insulating layers. This reduces parasitic capacitance and results in faster transistors.

3.4 Drawbacks

3.4.1 Introduction

So far, three-dimensional structures have been presented in a rather optimistic light. There are, however, a number of difficulties associated with both the manufacture and operation of three-dimensional circuits. The manufacturing difficulties include the provision of high quality semiconductor and wiring materials in the various layers, and reduced yield due to the increased number of processing steps. The operational difficulties are primarily electrical interference between layers and heat dissipation though the structure.

3.4.2 Materials

An important restriction on the composition of three-dimensional circuits is imposed by the techniques used to provide semiconducting layers. The recrystallisation technique involves the melting of polycrystalline silicon at a temperature of around 1450°C. The transient heat involved has two implications. First, overall yield can be reduced by the slight degradation of devices on underlying layers. This can be minimised by a thermal annealing step after each recrystallisation.

Second, and more importantly, the temperatures reached in the underlying layers during the recrystallisation process preclude the use of low melting point substances in these layers, particularly aluminium which melts at around 700°C. Higher melting point materials such as molybdenum, tungsten or silicides relieve the situation. Alternatively, solid phase silicon epitaxy involves much lower processing temperatures, and so imposes less severe thermal constraints on the composition of underlying layers. This also reduces the degree to which impurities are distributed in lower layers.

Another critical requirement is the planarisation of the surface after each layer is fabricated. Good planarisation is vital in order to achieve good quality crystal growth. Techniques have been developed to planarise the surface to within 0.1μm.

3.4.3   Yield

There are many possible defects which affect both bulk silicon and SOI technologies. For a particular method of manufacture, the distribution of defects acts as a measure of the quality of wafers produced. The defects correspond to inconsistencies in the crystal structure of the silicon, which affect devices created at such locations. The device may not function at all, leading to total circuit failure or intermittent behaviour, or the device may function with degraded electrical characteristics leading to a rejection of the device on performance grounds. Other defects are caused by the mis-alignment of mask steps, and the use of small geometries resulting in misaligned contacts, cracks, pinholes in oxides, shorts, opens and thin metal.

For a given chip area A and defect density D, the yield Y is the probability that a chip will function. Statistical models have been developed to predict the yield probability, based on assumptions about the distribution of defects. A simple model assumes point-like defects with a random, or Poisson distribution. The yield is simply the probability of zero defects P_0 and is given by

$$Y = P_0(AD) = e^{-AD}.$$

However, defects are not randomly distributed, and a more complex model is required. Mixed Poisson statistics were introduced to model yield in terms of a defect density function $f(D)$ [Murphy 64] and the general form is

$$Y = \int_0^\infty e^{-AD} f(D) dD.$$

A gamma approximation for the density function produces probabilities in good accordance with observations [Stapper 73], and a derived formula in widespread use is

$$Y = (1 + AD)^{-1}. \tag{3.1}$$

For three-dimensional circuits, the problem of yield is compounded with every extra level of transistors added to the process. In the best possible case, the yield of a stack of N layers each of area A would be the same as the yield of the equivalent area NA in a single layer. As with WSI, three-dimensional circuits with large total areas attract a very low yield. However, the problem is worse since upper layers of transistors are difficult to fabricate and are susceptible to defects due to lack of planarisation and deterioration of semiconductor quality. In addition, the defect count of the underlying layers may increase retrospectively during the thermal stress of fabricating the upper layers. The yield of a three-dimensional structure must be modelled in terms of the total number of mask and semiconductor deposition steps.

Modelling of overall yield in terms of the yields of each mask level in a conventional process is described in [Gandemer 88]. A specific yield for each level is modelled on equation 3.1, giving

$$Y_i = (1 + A_i D_i)^{-1}$$

where Y_i is the yield at level i, A_i is the area of the chip susceptible to the faults at this level, and D_i is the mean defect density. A level critical coefficient α_i is introduced to rearrange the yield in terms of the total chip area A, giving

$$Y_i = (1 + AD_i)^{-\alpha_i}.$$

The overall yield is then

$$Y = \prod_i Y_i = \prod_i (1 + AD_i)^{-\alpha_i}.$$

By assuming the same mean defect density D for each level, a simplified version is

$$Y = (1 + AD)^{-\alpha}$$

where

$$\alpha = \sum_i \alpha_i.$$

The values of D_i can be determined from the mask sets of a proposed layout, while the values of α_i are calculated from observed defect counts. Forming similar defect counts for every layer in a three-dimensional process would clearly enable an overall yield to be established. This discussion is continued in chapter eight.

3.4.4   Interference

Two sources of interference between wiring and components in a three-dimensional circuit are crosstalk and back-gating. Crosstalk is the electrical coupling of signals between insulated parallel conductors. In general, the amount of crosstalk depends on the amplitude of the signals, the physical separation of the conductors, the inductance or capacitance of the insulating material and the edge speed of the signal. This effect occurs in two-dimensional circuits, particularly in double metal processes where two planes of conductors are separated by an insulating layer typically $1\mu m$ thick.

The effect is usually quite unpronounced in digital circuits, and the principal method of limiting crosstalk is to arrange conductors in adjacent layers to run in perpendicular directions. In three dimensions, the addition of extra device and wiring layers is directly analogous to the two level metal case. The separation between the top level of conductors in the first device layer and the bottom of the semiconducting level of the second device layer is typically $1\mu m$. Similar techniques can be used to minimise crosstalk, and devices in the second layer can be arranged to be non-overlapping with devices in the first layer, and so on.

A second source of interference of particular relevance to three-dimensional circuits is the formation of a back-gate at the bottom of an upper transistor channel, controlled by the voltage of the lower layer. The threshold voltage of this back-gate depends upon the quality of the semiconductor crystal and of the semiconductor/insulator interface. The effect is quite small with materials of reasonable quality. The effect of the back-gate could be either to introduce a DC bias into the upper transistor or to introduce a frequency component from the lower layer and cause modulation in the upper layer. Crosstalk effects are greatly reduced in CMOS circuits which have a much greater noise immunity than the corresponding NMOS circuit. It may prove necessary to investigate the use of an earthed conducting layer to act as a shielding plate between active layers, though this would tend to increase the capacitance of the devices in the SOI layer.

3.4.5   Heat dissipation

For many types of bipolar transistor, the power consumption and consequent heat dissipation of large, fast circuits has always been a problem due to the high currents involved in transistor switching. It can also be a problem in VLSI MOS and CMOS circuits, due to the cumulative effects of large numbers of transistors each dissipating a small amount of power when switched. The power dissipation has a strong frequency relationship, as the frequency increases so does the power dissipation. The temperature of the chip and constituent transistors has a marked effect on the operating characteristics of the device. Junction temperatures of above 200°C usually result in catastrophic failure. Note that in general, as the temperature of the chip increases, the signal delays increase.

For two-dimensional circuits, heat is dissipated by conduction through the package to the air, and by the pins to the circuit board. The effectiveness of air cooling at dissipating the heat and maintaining acceptable junction temperatures can be increased by the use of multi-vaned heat sinks. These offer a greater surface area, and with forced air cooling provide a steeper temperature gradient. The power consumption is reduced at source by the use of small geometries and the corresponding smaller circuits. However, since any area saved by scaling is usually filled by more devices, the power consumption of a given area of circuit is liable to remain fairly constant. CMOS logic enjoys very low static power consumption due to the very high input impedances and the charge storing capabilities of the transistor gates. Dynamic switching currents account for much of the power dissipation. However, very high frequency or high density circuits can generate too much heat to be dissipated by conventional air cooling methods. A solution is to force cool the package with a high thermal capacity liquid under pressure, a technique has been used with success in the IBM Thermal Conduction Module [Oktay 82].

The potential for much more effective forced cooling techniques has been reported in [Tuckerman 81], [Sasaki 86]. It was shown that one of the chief impediments to conduction is the heat transfer coefficient between the substrate and the coolant. In a similar way to heat sinks, an increased substrate to coolant area would achieve greater dissipation. An effective way to achieve this is to make many microscopic cooling channels in the substrate itself (Figure 3.8(a)). A coolant forced through these channels can have a dramatic effect and a forty-fold increase in practical heat sinking capability is claimed. However, the extra manufacturing steps and the supply of coolant under pressure involve higher production, installation and operating costs.

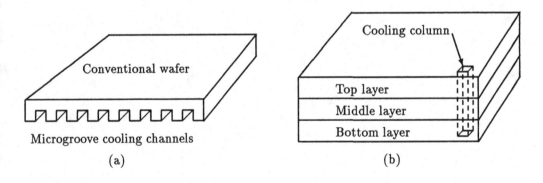

Conventional wafer

Microgroove cooling channels

(a)

Cooling column

Top layer

Middle layer

Bottom layer

(b)

Figure 3.8: Cooling channels

Silicon and silicon dioxide are fairly good thermal insulators, and a significant proportion of heat dissipated has conventionally been carried away by metal connections. In three dimensions, the problem of power dissipation becomes more acute since the use of metal connections will almost certainly be subject to restrictions. Furthermore, only the outer two levels are in physical contact with the surrounding encapsulation. For three or more layers, the heat dissipated by devices in internal levels must diffuse through intermediate levels to the outside. This clearly causes a temperature gradient and an adverse temperature build up in the centre is possible. The silicides mentioned earlier not only have high electrical conductance and mechanical stability but greater thermal conductance too.

A technique to assist the dissipation of heat in a three-dimensional circuit could be devised, similar to the forced substrate method. During the layout of each layer, areas could be systematically reserved, aligned throughout the layers. As one of the final fabrication steps, vertical channels are created through each reserved area, perhaps by reactive ion etching. These channels could be used to carry a coolant such as an inert gas under pressure. This would provide effective cooling directly at the sources of heat generation (Figure 3.8(b)).

There may be a profound effect on the whole integrated circuit industry since the advent of high-temperature superconductors. These materials may find use in the manufacture of integrated circuits, providing extremely low resistance conductors. This will enable circuits to operate much faster and with greatly reduced power dissipation due to the low loss in such conductors.

Chapter 4

Three-Dimensional Circuit Topology

4.1 Wiring schemes

4.1.1 Introduction

A number of limitations imposed by the technology of three-dimensional integration have been mentioned. These limitations restrict the total number of transistors and the number of layers in which transistors can be constructed. However, for a given number of layers the topology of circuit layout is most profoundly affected by the availability and quality of wiring both within and between the layers.

For the layout problem, the distribution of wiring is determined by the edges in the physical layout graph, which is the initially empty spatial grid in which edges are wires and vertices are transistors or gates. The logical circuit graph specifies the structural connectivity of the circuit in terms of nodes and signals. Since layout consists of embedding the logical circuit graph into the physical layout graph, the pattern of edges in the physical graph has an effect on the compactness of the embedding. Contact and wiring techniques are now discussed.

4.1.2   Contact techniques

A range of contact techniques are available for three-dimensional structures, providing direct connection between diffusion, gate and wiring regions. Conventional contact methods which are used for connections within a single layer of transistors can be applied to create direct connections between layers of transistors. With the butting contact, regions are connected by contact with the wiring material which is particularly useful when the signal connected is required elsewhere in the circuit. In particular, connection can be formed between the gate and diffusion regions of a single transistor (Figure 4.1(a)), or a pair of stacked transistors (Figure 4.1(b)) [Kawamura 83].

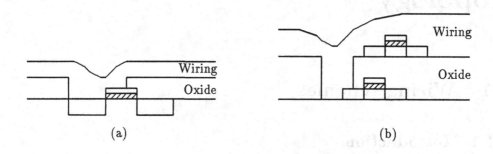

Figure 4.1: Butting contacts

The buried contact, a more sophisticated technique requiring an extra mask step, is suitable for connecting two regions without the need for a wiring contact. Figure 4.2(a) shows the connection of gate and diffusion in a single transistor. Part of the gate oxide is etched away prior to depositing the polysilicon layer. Electrical contact is made when the polysilicon layer is subsequently doped. Buried contacts can also be used to connect regions in two adjacent device layers. For example, the diffusions of two vertically stacked transistors can be connected directly by opening a contact hole in the separating insulator above the lower diffusion layer. When the upper silicon film is recrystallised and doped, connection is made (Figure 4.2(b)).

4.1.3   Intra-layer wiring

Connections within the same device layer can be provided with conventional contact and wiring techniques. As mentioned previously, the choice of material for wiring

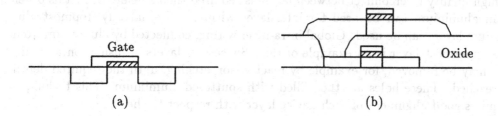

Figure 4.2: Buried contacts

may be restricted by the thermal stresses of the isolation process. In recrystallisation processes, temperatures of at least 1450°C are encountered in the vicinity of the recrystallising film. Aluminium is therefore unusable for metallisation within internal device layers for such processes. Note that the topmost device layer is not subject to any further adverse heating and may therefore contain aluminium.

High circuit connectivity requires readily available wiring for efficient layout. For random circuits in two-dimensional layouts this means at least two layers of interconnect. More advanced processes offer triple-layer metal/polysilicon combinations. However, in three-dimensional layouts this number of wiring levels is not necessarily required in every device layer. Direct contact between devices on adjacent layers reduces the need for explicit wiring, and one or two polysilicon/silicide layers can be sufficient for localised intra-layer wiring, with longer wire runs provided by a more global wiring scheme using metal layers on the topmost device layer. This is particularly true for integrated circuits with a small number of transistor layers, as was demonstrated by [Kawamura 84a].

4.1.4   Inter-layer wiring

Metallisation constraints within the horizontal plane also constrain the vertical wiring between device layers. If aluminium wiring cannot be used on an internal device layer then it cannot be used for the isolated connection between device layers. This precludes butting contacts involving aluminium, at least between internal layers. Fortunately, much can be achieved by buried style contacts between diffusions and gates of vertically adjacent transistors, since buried contacts can be made between any combinations of diffusion and polysilicon levels in adjacent layers. Connections between devices on several layers can be formed by threading such contacts through device layers, provided suitable placements can be found to facilitate this.

If high quality interconnect between layers is required then silicides or metals other than aluminium can be used for inter-layer wiring. Alternatively, topmost aluminium layers can be used. Global intra-layer wiring, connected by aluminium from the uppermost layer is an example of this. Successive layers of insulation and silicon may be removed, for example by reactive ion etching, until the required depth is reached. These holes are then filled with sputtered aluminium. This technique requires good alignment of each device layer with respect to the others.

4.1.5   Power wiring

The power supply to devices is usually arranged in low resistivity metal wiring. Polysilicon wiring is unsuitable for any great distance because of its high resistivity. As geometries become smaller, the charges and voltages involved become less, and the power requirements of individual transistors are reduced. However, the total number of transistors in an integrated circuit will tend to increase and higher switching speeds may be involved. Therefore the total power requirements may remain unchanged.

An example of a three-dimensional power and ground distribution is shown in Figure 4.3. Short polysilicon or longer silicide power tracks on each layer can be fed from a vertical metal power lines. The distribution of the vertical power lines depends on the suitability of the inter-layer wiring material as a carrier of power. More conductive, higher melting point wiring materials within each layer would require fewer vertical feeds.

4.2   A classification

4.2.1   Three factors

A classification of the topology of three-dimensional structures in terms of the distribution of transistors and wiring in three dimensions is presented. This is useful for a number of reasons. First, by viewing a class of topologies in terms of the technological constraints of fabricating circuits within that class, it is possible to gauge the benefits in circuit layout which result from extra technological effort. For example, providing additional wiring capability at each transistor plane may not improve layout enough to justify the greater complexity and reduced yield. Second,

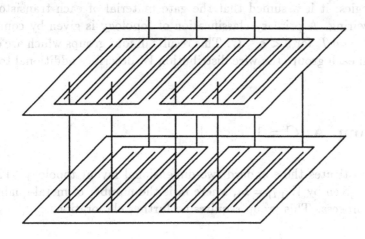

Figure 4.3: Three-dimensional power distribution

a given type of circuit will be most efficiently embedded into the physical graph of one or more topologies. This helps to assess the uses of a particular group. For example, memory and random circuits have different requirements for the positions of devices and wiring. Third, certain design methods impose particular constraints on the topology of the structure. For example, gate array methods require that a good degree of customisation is readily achievable with the completion of a few simple mask steps.

It is useful to define three factors to classify the topology of three-dimensional structures. First, the number of layers of cells in the complete structure will be denoted by C. Second, the number of transistor levels involved in a cell at layer c will be denoted by T_c. In the constructions fabricated so far, the total number of transistor levels has been small, which is reflected by the magnitude of

$$\sum_{c=1}^{C} T_c.$$

A third factor is the type and availability of wiring. The distribution of metal quality wiring throughout the structure is denoted by $W_{(c,t)}$ which is the number of metal-quality wiring planes available at cell layer c, transistor level t. A similar expression for the total number of wire layers is

$$\sum_{c=1}^{C} \sum_{t=1}^{T_c} W_{(c,t)}.$$

For all topologies, it is assumed that the gate material of each transistor level is available for wiring. A primary classification of topology is given by combinations of the values C and T_c for $0 < c \leq C$. This results in four groups which are described below. Within each group, the wire distribution W describes additional topological constraints.

4.2.2   Group A: $C = 1, T_C = 1$

This group constitutes the standard two-dimensional layout topology. The wiring distribution is given by $W_{(1,1)} = m$, where m is the number of metal-quality wiring planes in the process. This group requires no further elaboration.

4.2.3   Group B: $C = 1, T_C > 1$

This group represents structures with a single layer of multiple level cells, each cell having the same number of levels. For a small number of levels, it is sufficient to provide upper level metallisation only, that is

$$W_{(1,t)} = \begin{cases} m & \text{if } t = T_C \\ 0 & \text{otherwise} \end{cases}$$

Note that connections between lower levels can be accommodated with the contact techniques described earlier. With only two transistor levels a large number of different cells can be constructed using simple internal contacts [Kawamura 84a]. Two-level cells offer an immediate saving in total area and a corresponding reduction in total wire length over the equivalent single-level cell. There are two reasons for this. First, the cell itself is more compact since direct contact between transistor regions on the two levels replaces longer wire connections. This also speeds up the cell. Second, since the base area of each cell is reduced by about half, the cells themselves can be arranged in a more compact layout saving interconnect between cells. This further speeds up the circuit.

Compared with the corresponding single level bulk counterpart, performance and density gains of around 20% are predicted for a two level SOI flip-flop with one upper metallisation plane, $W_{(1,2)} = 1$ [ESPRIT 86]. Roughly half of this improvement is due to the use of SOI technology. Further gains of around 10% were predicted for a layout with two upper planes of metallisation, $W_{(1,2)} = 2$. However, these

predictions were based on proposed layouts which did not make use of buried inter-
level contacts and more compact design is perhaps possible. Furthermore, the study
did not consider improvements in layout at a higher level. In particular, since two-
level cells have a reduced base area, they can be packed together more densely
and interconnected with less wiring material. These savings are additional to those
within the cell.

Processes using a single layer of multi-level cells are the simplest extension of existing
two-dimensional SOI, and the interest shown in this type of three-dimensional structure indicates that it may be amongst the first commercially available homogeneous
three-dimensional integrated circuits. A relevant question is 'how many transistor
levels to use?'. An answer lies in considering the contents of each cell. A simple
inverter requires at most two levels. It can be seen that two levels are sufficient
for a large range of combinational gates and simple flip-flops. A larger number of
levels is only of use for considerably more complex cells. This is then wasteful for
simpler cells which must nevertheless contain the same number of levels. Greater
utilisation of highly three-dimensional structures is found in other groups, and not
by expanding the cell vertically. It is expected that in practice the number of useful
levels per cell will be two or three.

4.2.4   Group C: $C > 1, T_c = 1$ for all $0 < c \leq C$

This group represents structures composed of a number of layers of single level cells.
Arbitrarily sized blocks of cells may be constrained to lie wholly within a device
layer, or may be spread over a number of layers. If the contents of a block lie
within one layer, then at some level in the hierarchy of the design there may be a
functional separation between the device layers [Inou 86]. The functional separation
may be emphasised by technological separation, leading to the heterogeneous three-
dimensional structures mentioned earlier [Geis 86].

The potential for inter-layer vertical connection on a massive scale is demonstrated
in [Hite 85], and short vertical bus structures with functions gathered around the
bus on each layer can be imagined particularly in designs with parallel structures
[Grinberg 84]. At least one metal-quality wiring plane is required at each device
layer, that is $W_{(c,1)} = 1$ for all $0 < c \leq C$, particularly for structures with mixed
technologies where the inter-layer contact techniques may not be applicable.

4.2.5   Group D: $C > 1$

This is the most general group, represented by a number of layers with a distribution of device levels which satisfies $T_c > 1$ for some $0 < c \leq C$. A uniform distribution would correspond to a structure with a number of layers of multiple level cells. A non-uniform distribution might correspond to a layer of multiple-level cells fabricated above a single level layer of devices in the substrate. In each case, the wiring distribution would need to be $W_{(c,T_c)} > 0$ for all $0 < c \leq C$.

4.3   Design methods

4.3.1   Custom

Three-dimensional custom design is a daunting prospect. Manual layout of large numbers of transistors in three dimensions is difficult, even for just two transistor levels. As well as the difficulties of spatial conception for the designer, extra demands are placed on the graphical depiction of such circuits using conventional layout editor style design tools and displays. In fact, this is already seen as a problem with large two-dimensional circuits. It is almost certainly the case that large custom designs in three dimensions will require a much greater, perhaps total, degree of automated synthesis and implementation.

Where functions are separated and contained wholly within one device layer (group C), conventional floor planning can be used on each layer in turn. Assignment of functions to layers may be dictated by the provision of different technologies, or may be freely chosen. Even with a small number of layers, the ability to route buses vertically and cluster connected blocks around them could have a dramatic effect. Compare the two- and three-dimensional floor plans of Figure 4.4(a) and Figure 4.4(b). Each block in the three-dimensional circuit has the same layout as in the two-dimensional circuit, and offers no savings in device area. However, the richer topology of the three-dimensional floor plan allows assignment of blocks such that vertical buses relieve the congestion of the inter-block routing and save area. Since the vertical separation is small, such buses are greatly reduced in length and may be faster.

If a function is distributed between several layers, the blocks of a floor plan become three-dimensional objects. The requirement to display and edit such a floor plan

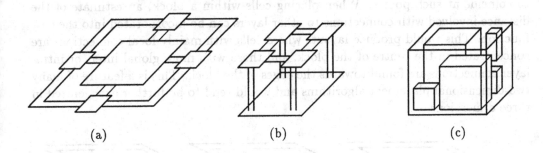

(a)   (b)   (c)

Figure 4.4: Floor plans

places new demands on layout editing. Three-dimensional graphical display, perhaps with hidden line removal and fast movement of viewpoint would be required. With a two-dimensional floor plan, blocks are usually constrained to be rectangular to simplify the layout process. In three dimensions, the blocks can be similarly constrained to be cuboid (Figure 4.4(c)). However, this introduces further display problems. For example, cuboids can be partially or totally obscured from a particular viewpoint. Worse than this, a cuboid can be completely obscured from all external viewpoints. Slices through the layers, either vertically or horizontally would be needed in this case.

4.3.2 Standard cell

The standard cell design method can be applied to three-dimensional integration using a number of layout topologies. At least one wiring plane per cell layer is required to allow channels to be used in a conventional manner. A single layer of multiple level cells (group B) does not require any new layout techniques. However, multiple layers of cells (groups C and D) require three-dimensional placement and routing procedures. A number of approaches to standard cell design in three dimensions are parameterised by the availability of the vertical connection.

In the simplest case, the devices and connections of each floor plan block are constrained to lie wholly within one layer. This enables each block and therefore each entire layer to be placed and routed using conventional standard cell placement and channel routing methods. A small number of vertical connections are gathered together at a number of points in the global routing space to form vertical channels between layers (Figure 4.5(a)). The layout of adjacent layers is therefore constrained to coincide at such points. When placing cells within a block, an estimate of the distance involved with connections to other layers can be incorporated into the cost function. This would produce layouts where cells with mainly local connections are concentrated in the centre of the block, and those with more global inter- or intra-layer connections are found towards the edges of the block. This is a feature of many two-dimensional placement algorithms and would tend to be further exaggerated in three dimensions.

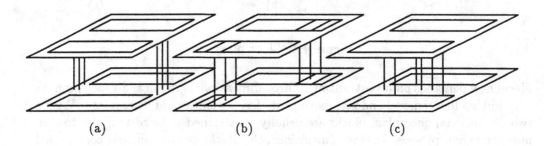

$$(a) \qquad\qquad (b) \qquad\qquad (c)$$

Figure 4.5: Vertical routing channels

A greater degree of vertical connection can be provided with 'feedup' cells, analogous to the two-dimensional feedthrough cell (Figure 4.5(b)). Vertical routing is achieved by placement of two such feedup cells at the same horizontal coordinate in adjacent cell layers. This clearly imposes additional constraints on the relative layout of the layers, requiring some degree of overlapping between the strips of cells in blocks on adjacent layers. If channels are also constrained to overlap, more general vertical connections can be provided by vertical vias between device layers at arbitrary points within channels (Figure 4.5(c)). These could be provided 'on demand' by the routing phase. When choosing cell placements, estimates of the distance between cells should be calculated on the basis of their relative three-dimensional positions. This leads to reduced channel densities and improved routing over the simple vertical wiring method, and a consequent saving in materials and circuit speed-up.

4.3.3   Gate array

A true gate array must be a prefabricated stock component which is readily cus-tomised with the addition of a few mask steps. This typically involves the connection by metallisation of a pre-defined grid of cells. Note that customisation may involve the specification of wiring connections within a cell, giving the ability to design circuits with a number of cell types. In three dimensions there is an apparent problem in that all underlying layers must be pre-fabricated to a high degree, and therefore the total number of useful layers in a gate array is limited. The topology of group B suggests a suitable implementation of a three-dimensional gate array. By constructing a cell on a number of layers, immediate savings in materials can be expected. Two level metal provides further opportunities for improving routing. Further increases in circuit density for gate arrays are possible by adding extra layers (group D - uniform distribution). However, these layers still require connection by metallisation from above. This could be achieved by offsetting cells in two device layers. The benefit would be a factor of two increase in density at most (Figure 4.6(a)).

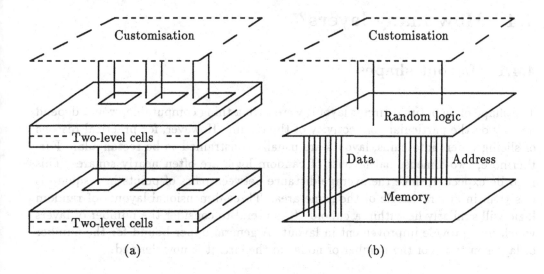

Figure 4.6: Three-dimensional gate arrays

There are other benefits of three-dimensional circuits while still adhering to the strict gate array scheme. One example is to have an uppermost layer of cells, possibly multilevel, built on top of a layer of memory cells (group D - non-uniform distribution). Many larger digital designs call for the use of registers, queues and memory. When quick turnround is required, such systems are often designed as a chip set with random logic implemented in a gate array and regular structures provided by stock components. By including some of the most used regular circuits on a lower device layer, the benefits of a single chip solution are available. Buffering between the integrated circuits and the external connections introduces significant delays, and so the fewer chips involved in a system the better.

In a simple case, a single byte wide memory might be provided. Figure 4.6(b) shows a possible arrangement of this. A range of different base layers can be offered by the manufacturer, but the general purpose nature of gate arrays will limit the useful combinations of base layer components. In a more complex case, the base layer could contain larger systems such as complete processors. The upper layer could contain a mix of random logic array and physical sensors. Thus complete systems of great complexity and power could be customised with the simple techniques of gate array layout.

4.4   How many layers?

4.4.1   Layout shapes

The shape of an optimal circuit layout, were such a thing computable, would depend heavily on the particular connectivity of the circuit. However, for practical reasons of slicing wafers into chips, layouts are usually constrained to be rectangular. Furthermore, two-dimensional layouts of random logic are often nearly square. This is to be expected, since the average distance between pairs of points in a square is less than in any rectangle of the same area. Three-dimensional layouts of random logic will similarly lie within a cuboid. It is useful to consider the number of layers which may provide improvement in layout. A general upper bound for the number of layers in terms of the number of nodes in the circuit is now derived.

4.4.2   An upper bound

Consider a logical graph of N nodes which can be perfectly embedded in a three-dimensional rectangular physical grid with x vertices in the x-axis, y vertices in the y-axis and z vertices in the z-axis. A perfect embedding is one where the nodes and connections of the logical graph can be assigned to the vertices and edges of the physical grid such that every vertex corresponds to a node, and every connection corresponds to a set of edges threading through the vertices. Note that the dimensions of the cuboid are related by

$$N = xyz. \tag{4.1}$$

Assume unit separation between vertices in the x-axis, separation a in the y-axis and separation b in the z-axis. An upper bound on the total possible amount of wiring material, w_3, in the three-dimensional grid is given by

$$w_3 = yz(x-1) + axz(y-1) + bxy(z-1). \qquad (4.2)$$

This can be used as a measure of the compactness of the layout. Substituting for z using equation 4.1 gives

$$w_3 = N - \frac{N}{x} + aN - \frac{aN}{y} + bN - bxy.$$

The layout will be most compact when w_3 is minimum. To find the values of x, y for which this holds, the partial derivatives are formed

$$\frac{\partial w}{\partial x} = \frac{N}{x^2} - by = 0, \quad \text{and} \quad \frac{\partial w}{\partial y} = \frac{aN}{y^2} - bx = 0$$

giving

$$x^3 = \frac{N}{ab}, \quad y^3 = \frac{a^2 N}{b}, \quad z^3 = \frac{b^2 N}{a}.$$

Substituting into 4.2 gives

$$\min w_3 = (1 + a + b)N - 3(ab)^{\frac{1}{3}} N^{\frac{2}{3}}. \qquad (4.3)$$

The same circuit in a two-dimensional grid would require at least the wire length of a perfect two-dimensional embedding

$$w_2 = (1 + a)N - 2a^{\frac{1}{2}} N^{\frac{1}{2}},$$

plus the wire length of the extra vertical connections which must now be routed through additional vertices

$$w_{\text{vertical}} = xyz = N.$$

Therefore the wire length of the two-dimensional layout can be no better than

$$\min w_2 = (1 + a)N - 2a^{\frac{1}{2}} N^{\frac{1}{2}} + \min(1, a)N. \qquad (4.4)$$

In the orthonormal case, setting $a = b = 1$ in equation 4.3 and equation 4.4 we have

$$w_2 = 3N - 2N^{\frac{1}{2}}$$
$$w_3 = 3N - 3N^{\frac{1}{3}}.$$

In practice, the two-dimensional layout will be much worse than this since the perfect two-dimensional embedding cannot correspond to the horizontal component of the perfect three-dimensional embedding. A more interesting case, setting $a = 1$, $b = 0.1$ gives

$$
\begin{aligned}
w_2 &= 3N - 2N^{\frac{1}{2}} \\
w_3 &\approx 2.1N - 1.4N^{\frac{2}{3}},
\end{aligned}
$$

which is more favourable for three-dimensions.

4.5   Other work

4.5.1   Theoretical

A study of the two-dimensional layout of rearrangeable permutation networks is presented in [Thompson 79]. Rearrangeable permutation networks have the general topology of a set of sorting nodes with wide application. An eight-rearrangeable permutation network is shown in Figure 4.7. It was shown that the area of the optimal circuit layout of an N-rearrangeable permutation graph is proportional to N^2, and the maximum wire length is proportional to $N/\log_2 N$. This was achieved by recursively forming bisections of the graph and formulating a method of wiring between each pair of subgraphs involving a calculable area at each level. The symmetric properties of permutation graphs facilitate this and also contribute to the argument that the layout is optimal. A study of the three-dimensional layout of such graphs is presented in [Rosenberg 83], in which similar techniques result in volume proportional to $N^{\frac{3}{2}}$ and maximum wire length proportional to $N^{\frac{1}{2}}$.

Results for a more general class of three-dimensional circuit layout are reported in [Leighton 85]. Is essence, the work derives close upper and lower bounds on the volume and maximum wire length with which circuits can be realised in a multilayer medium. Furthermore, the work shows how to transform two-dimensional layouts into more efficient three-dimensional layouts. Two models are investigated for layout. The one-active-layer model uses the third dimension for wiring only, while the many-active-layer model allows arbitrary placement of devices throughout the layers. An outline of the methods and results is presented below.

The models employ a rectangular grid of vertices and edges as before, but with five restrictions:

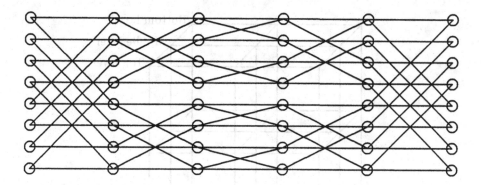

Figure 4.7: An eight-rearrangeable permutation network

- Every vertex has at most three incident edges,

- Every edge connects at most two vertices,

- A vertex at a layer change contains a single wire segment,

- All edges have unit length,

- Every vertex has unit area.

The method for deriving the bounds for the one-active-layer model follows from considering a projection of a three-dimensional grid onto the plane (Figure 4.8). Each diagonal edge in the projection is removed by rerouting the wire segment it contains through one of the two adjacent right-angles. Since these diagonal edges change layers, only one wire is present at the vertices on each layer. Therefore, at least one of the adjacent right-angles already contains an electrically equivalent wire segment and so the rerouting is always possible. By considering the grid constraints in the vicinity of such a layer collapse, a reverse transformation can be established. For the one-active-layer model it was shown that the volume V satisfies

$$(AN)^{\frac{1}{2}} \leq V \leq \log_2 \left(\frac{N^2}{A} \right) (AN)^{\frac{1}{2}} \tag{4.5}$$

and the maximum length of any wire W satisfies

$$\left(\frac{A}{N} \right)^{\frac{1}{2}} \leq W \leq N^{\frac{1}{2}} \tag{4.6}$$

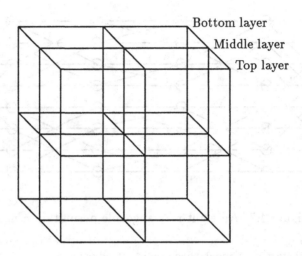

Figure 4.8: A two-dimensional projection of a three layer grid

where N is the number of devices and A is the area of the two-dimensional layout.

The method for deriving the bounds for the many-active layer model is substantially more complex, and is a development of the earlier work on the graph bisection of rearrangeable permutation networks. A graph G has a decomposition tree $(F_0, F_1, \ldots, F_r)$ if G can be decomposed into two subgraphs G_0 and G_1 by removing F_0 edges from G, each G_0 and G_1 can be decomposed by removing F_1 edges and so on, until $G_{2^r}, \ldots, G_{2^{r+1}-1}$ are either empty or contain a single vertex. A decomposition tree where F decreases at a uniform rate ρ is called a ρ-bifurcator of size F. It has been shown that in the two-dimensional case, finding a small $2^{\frac{1}{2}}$-bifurcator for the graph is a key to an efficient layout [Leighton 82]. For the many-active-layer three-dimensional case, the analogy is to find a small $2^{\frac{2}{3}}$-bifurcator. Recasting the results of the three-dimensional bifurcation in terms of the results of a two-dimensional bifurcation gives the following bounds

$$A^{\frac{3}{4}} \leq V \leq (AN)^{\frac{1}{2}} \qquad (4.7)$$

$$\left(\frac{A}{N}\right)^{\frac{1}{2}} \leq W \leq (AN)^{\frac{1}{6}}.$$

One surprising conclusion was that within the framework of the models, the many-active-layer layouts do not appear to be significantly better than the one-active-layer layouts. The upper bounds of equation 4.5 and equation 4.7 differ by only a logarithmic factor $\log_2(\frac{N^2}{A})$. This is perhaps due to some of the grid restrictions. The most unreasonable restriction is that all vertices have the same area. In particular, vertices containing a layer change have the same area as vertices which contain a device. This is wasteful since the smallest device under consideration would be a transistor which has many times the area of an inter-layer via. The restriction that a vertex changing layers contains a single wire segment is necessary for the purposes of the proof, but unreasonable as a component of the overall framework. If all vertices must have the same area, then each layer changing vertex has spare capacity for routing around the layer change.

It may be the case that high vertex degrees are better treated in three dimensions. The restriction that every vertex is incident to at most three wires does not exploit the three-dimensional topology. Finally, the isometry assumption introduces further degradation of the results. Modelling a reduced inter-layer distance is not a purely clerical matter of scaling the result, since it would be expected that the optimal three-dimensional circuit layout would occupy a different number of layers. This is implied by equation 4.3. These issues are addressed in chapter eight, where the results of practical layout experiments formed by a system designed to work on a similar grid framework are presented.

4.5.2 Practical

There is little work on practical three-dimensional layout described in the literature, ten years after the first JMOS devices were fabricated. It is perhaps thought that three-dimensional circuits will be on a small number of levels and will either be functionally separated (group C), or composed of multi-level cells (group B). As mentioned earlier, these types of three-dimensional structures can be designed using simply modified two-dimensional layout systems. Such layout systems which may have been adapted for three-dimensional use have not, in general, warranted description. Because layout on a larger number of levels is not yet thought practical, no attention has been given to random logic layout techniques and the improvement which might be gained.

However, a three-dimensional design methodology is described in [Hoefflinger 84]. The methodology is specific to a two-level, joint gate CMOS technology, and is a set of interactive graphics tools which embody four levels of design abstraction. At the technology level, a cross section of material planes is displayed in either X or Y directions. This is a stylised subset of the technology details. At the mask level, the two levels of process masks are superimposed. This is confusing, even with different colour assignments for the different device levels. At the transistor level, the joint gate CMOS structure is represented as shown in Figure 4.9(b).

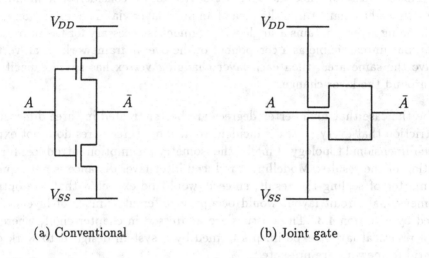

(a) Conventional   (b) Joint gate

Figure 4.9: Transistor level notations

The logic level description enables checks for topological congruence with the other design levels to be made, but the symbols used do not convey any of the three-dimensional nature of the underlying structures. Since pairs of complementary transistors form the basis of CMOS logic design, joint gate CMOS pairs become the basic unit of layout. Layout is reduced to the standard two-dimensional problem augmented by the customisation of each pair of transistors by specifying contacts between the metallisation, joint gate, and source and drain regions.

Chapter 5

Three-Dimensional Cell Tessellation

5.1 Layout by abutment

5.1.1 Introduction

The previous two chapters have outlined the technology enabling three-dimensional circuits to be constructed, and have examined some topologies which might result from the application of such technology. Some of the potential benefits of three-dimensional integration have been mentioned. These benefits are expected largely as a result of reduced wire length and device separation, and of the inherently richer connection topologies of three-dimensional circuits as shown in the two- and three-dimensional layouts of a half-adder circuit. The work by Leighton and Rosenberg on layout within a three-dimensional grid does not present a particularly optimistic view of three-dimensional circuits. This is primarily because of the restrictive assumptions in the adopted layout model which are necessary for the method of analysis employed.

It is the aim of this chapter to introduce a method of performing three-dimensional layout which will be the vehicle for a range of experiments. The method involves the postulation of a library of three-dimensional cells with particular geometric properties and the layout of circuits by combining the cells in a novel manner. It will be shown how the method can be used to perform layout in a number of ways, with a range of connection topologies. The chapter concludes with the physical design of logic cells which could form the basis of a practical system. Dimensions extracted from these cell designs will be used to scale the results of the layout experiments described in the next chapter.

5.1.2   Smaller wiring spaces

For two-dimensional integrated circuits, enhanced process capabilities can result in reduced feature sizes leading to smaller transistors and thinner wires. For example, in standard cell design the area of each row of cells is reduced since transistors can now be packed more densely and so each cell occupies less area. Similarly, thinner wires result in physically smaller routing channels, which is consistent with the expected reduction in the total amount of wiring material. However, the necessary routing channel density in terms of wires per channel remains unaltered.

With the richer, more varied connection topologies offered by three-dimensional integration a reduction in the logical density of the wiring spaces can also be expected. In the limit, direct connection is possible between the faces of adjacent, abutting cells. The juxtaposition of cells in three dimensions enhances the possibilities for connection through abutment by presenting a greater choice of cell faces to which wires can be assigned than the two-dimensional case. In three dimensions it may be that substantial amounts of the circuit connectivity can be satisfied by the suitable choice of abutting cells.

The layout method described below has been specifically designed to embrace the notion of direct connection by cell abutment. In this way, the method has the capability to explore layouts utilising direct connection where the best case three-dimensional layout involves such layout patterns. It is worth noting a common example of connection by abutment in conventional two-dimensional layouts where power supply and common clocking signals are often arranged to run along a row of cells which are designed to connect in this fashion. This compactness of connectivity can be further explored in the three-dimensional abutment scheme.

5.1.3   Basic abutment principles

The basic principles of layout by abutment will now be established. Layout by abutment consists wholly of the physical abutment of three-dimensional cells chosen from a suitably defined library. The cells are considered to be contained within bounding convex polyhedra, and are three-dimensional in the sense that they may connect through any of the faces of the polyhedra. Note that it is not necessary to consider the internal layout of the cell at this stage.

The cell library has two important properties. First, all cells in the library are geometrically homogeneous, that is each cell is the same shape and size. This is a necessary property for the prototype layout system described in the next chapter, which requires all cells to have the same number of faces. Second, all cells have uniform locations of interconnection points through the cell faces. This property ensures that all combinations of cells can be abutted.

The library contains two types of cell. A cell is considered to be *active* if it contains a circuit element such as a logic gate. Cells which contain only connections between faces are considered to be *passive*. In essence, the layout process consists of assigning connected nodes of the circuit to appropriately chosen adjacent cells such that connecting signals can be allocated to pairs of faces which abut. A cell may have unused connections. At any point, such unused connections can be used for wiring purposes, either for extra connections to signals already present in the cell or, where more than one connection is available, for additional 'over the cell' wiring. In effect, the cell is replaced by a similar but more specific cell. It is assumed that for a given choice of logic function, all configurations of cells containing the function are represented in the library, including configurations which utilise any spare connection capacity.

For large random logic circuits, it will not be generally possible to find assignments of nodes to cells such that the entire circuit is connected in this fashion. Passive cells are introduced as a means of providing additional wiring capability, and can be freely mixed with active cells creating areas for routing. The relationship between abutment and other layout methods will be discussed later, when abutment is considered as one process in the context of a broader system of layout.

5.2   Abutting cell shapes

5.2.1   Solid tessellation

A consequence of the above method of layout is that the geometrically homogeneous cells must have the additional property of solid tessellation, or 'filling space'. The term tessellation is normally used to refer to two-dimensional tiling of the plane, though interestingly the word originates from the Latin word *tessella* - a small stone cube. The connection topology of a cell is defined by the number and orientation of the faces. Since there is a wide range of different cells which tessellate space, there are many different connection topologies which can be explored with the abutment model. The classical groups of convex solids are described below. They are distinguished by the degree of congruence of the edges, faces and vertices of the solid. Particular mention is made of those solids which tessellate space and which are therefore candidates for libraries of abutting cells.

5.2.2   Platonic solids

There are five Platonic or regular solids, all of which were known to the Greeks. The solids occur in nature, either as crystals or as microscopic marine animals. Each solid is completely regular, with congruence between edges, between faces and between vertices. The five solids are distinguished by the number of faces (Table 5.1).

Name	*Face shape*	*Faces*	*Vertices*
Tetrahedron	Equilateral triangle	4	4
Cube or hexahedron	Square	6	8
Octahedron	Equilateral triangle	8	6
Dodecahedron	Pentagon	12	20
Icosahedron	Equilateral triangle	20	12

Table 5.1: The five Platonic solids

The cube is the only regular solid which tessellates space (Figure 5.1(a)). It can be shown that each of the other four Platonic solids is incapable of tessellating space by examining the angle between adjacent faces. The cube is the simplest and perhaps most useful cell shape. The topology of the connections between faces is clearly the same as a regular orthogonal grid, which is the basis for the standard layout framework. Grids which are topologically equivalent to the face connectivity of abutting cells are discussed later. Furthermore it will be shown how such cells can be constructed with planar transistors and vertical inter-layer vias.

5.2.3 Archimedean solids

There are thirteen Archimedean solids. Many of the Archimedean solids can be constructed by truncating the vertices of Platonic or other Archimedean solids. For example, the truncated octahedron is obtained by cutting each vertex of an octahedron, leaving six square vertex figures connecting eight hexagonal faces (Figure 5.1(b)). The truncated octahedron, quite remarkably, is one of a number of Archimedean solids which tessellates space. It is not at all obvious how this solid could be physically represented as a cell, but the novel connection topology offered is noted.

Another Archimedean solid which tessellates space is the rhombic dodecahedron (Figure 5.1(c)). This is most easily visualised by considering space tessellated with cubes alternately coloured black and white. Consider each white cube to be composed of six square based pyramids with the centre of the white cube as the common vertex. The surface of the rhombic dodecahedron is defined by the surface of the six white pyramids which surround a black cube. The resulting solid has twelve rhombic faces, and is easily seen to tessellate from this method of construction. Connecting through the faces of this solid is equivalent to connecting along lines drawn from the centre of a cube through the midpoint of each edge, that is a cube connected to its twelve edge adjacent neighbours. It is possible to imagine a cell with a planar functional element which exhibits the required connectivity both in the plane, and to the two adjacent planes.

5.2.4 Pyramids

Any regular polygon can form the base of a pyramid. An e edge polygon forms an $e + 1$ face pyramid. The only such pyramid which tessellates space is the square based pyramid with height equal to half the side of the square (Figure 5.1(d)). Six such pyramids combine to form a cube, as used in the construction of the rhombic dodecahedron. The connection topology of the rhombic dodecahedron can be em-

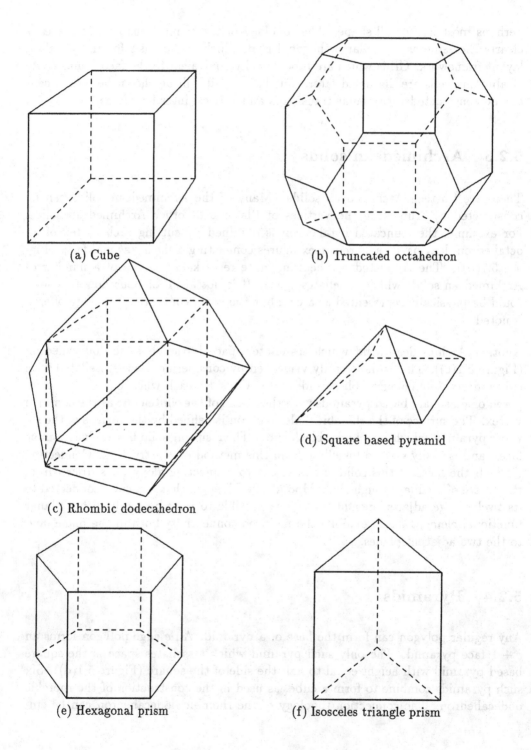

(a) Cube

(b) Truncated octahedron

(c) Rhombic dodecahedron

(d) Square based pyramid

(e) Hexagonal prism

(f) Isosceles triangle prism

Figure 5.1: Tessellating solids

bedded in the connection topology of the pyramid. However, the finer granularity of pyramid cell connection topology makes the design of a cell at this level more difficult.

5.2.5   Prisms

Any polygon can be the base of a prism, where each side of the prism is a rectangle. Using polygons which tessellate in two-dimensions, prisms can be formed which tessellate in three dimensions. An e edge polygon will form an $e + 2$ face prism. Examples of polygons forming tessellating prisms include the equilateral triangle (Figure 5.1(e)), and the hexagon (Figure 5.1(f)). This potentially large group is highly applicable to the design of three-dimensional abutting cells. By designing cells with the polygonal faces aligned with planes of transistors, the connections between rectangular faces of abutting cells can be assigned to suitably angled wires in those planes. Connection between polygonal faces of abutting cells can be assigned to simple vertical vias at some point within the polygonal faces of the cells.

5.3   Layout examples

5.3.1   Grid equivalence

A number of examples of layout by abutment using cells based on tessellating solids is now described. In each case, the connection topology of the particular shape of cell is highlighted by considering an equivalent grid representation. An equivalent grid of a cell is formed by representing the cell as a node in the grid and the connections to adjacent cells as wires radiating from the node to the point of contact at the abutting faces (Figure 5.2).

For purposes of geometric simplification an equivalent grid can be modified by altering the relative positions of nodes and the lengths of wires. This can always be done provided the topology of the grid is unaltered. Note that the distance between the centres of cells is no longer given by the length of the wires in the grid, and wires may have weights attached to reflect their true distances. For example, consider the equivalent grid of the hexagon based prisms shown in Figure 5.3.

In the following layout examples, the assignment of gates and signals to abutting

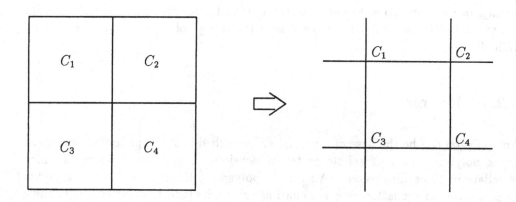

Figure 5.2: The cube equivalent grid

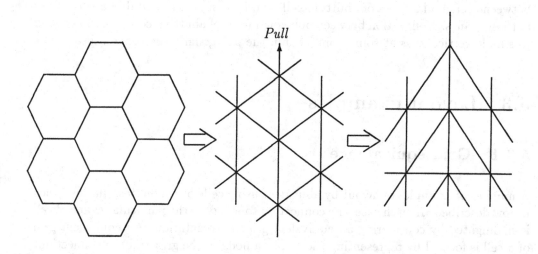

Figure 5.3: The hexagon prism equivalent grid

cells and faces is done by hand, and is not intended to be optimal. Furthermore, it is assumed that the supply of power to the cells is provided separately and does not use any part of the grid equivalent. The examples are presented in order of increasing cell connectivity, and only simple solids which have a readily identifiable cell structure are considered.

5.3.2   Equilateral triangle based prisms

This prism is one of the simplest solids which tessellate space. With only five faces, the number of wiring possibilities for a cell modelled on this prism is restricted. Passive cells allow at most two electrically distinct wires to be routed, and there are five logically different wiring possibilities. Figure 5.4 depicts two possible orientations of these cells with respect to the XY planes of transistors, together with their equivalent grids. The choice of transistor plane influences the orientation of the interconnection topology because of the asymmetry of the cells. In particular, a feedback loop requires six cells in the XY plane of Figure 5.4(a), but only four in the XY plane of Figure 5.4(b).

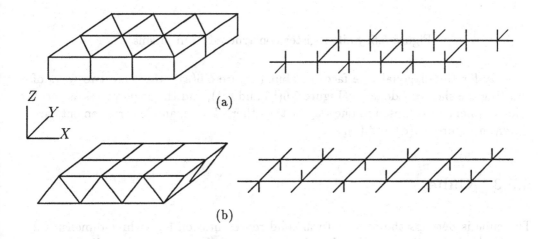

(a)

(b)

Figure 5.4: Equilateral triangle based prisms

If the library of cell functions includes a simple flip-flop, then the design possibilities are greatly enhanced, but at the obvious expense of cell volume. For example, a shift register can be constructed from flip-flop cells as in Figure 5.5. Note that both the length and the width of the shift register can be extended as required simply by abutment. Abutment at the triangular faces determines the width of the shift register, and these faces contain the clock signal. Abutment at the rectangular faces determines the length of the shift register and such faces contain the data paths through the register.

In fact, any triangle based prism will tessellate space, but the grid equivalent is not always regular. Consider a right-angle triangle based prism. Although there is only

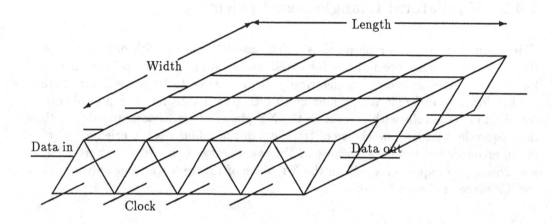

Figure 5.5: Shift register constructed from prisms

one way for the diagonal side faces to abut (Figure 5.6(a)), there are two ways of abutting the shorter side faces (Figure 5.6(b) and (c)), and the grid evolves as short side abutments are chosen in one way or the other. Two example arrangements are shown in Figure 5.6(d) and (e).

5.3.3   Cubes

The cube is perhaps the most natural solid representation for a three-dimensional cell, having a familiar orthogonal grid equivalent. Indeed, even in two-dimensions, cells are only normally considered to be rectangular. With six faces, the passive cell is capable of routing three electrically distinct wires, and there are ten logically different wiring possibilities. Active cells may contain simple combinational functions with say five inputs and one output. At this level of cell complexity, circuit elements such as flip-flops and latches must be constructed discretely from combinational cells. A fundamental topological feature of such elements which store information is a feedback loop which requires four cube shaped cells.

A set-reset latch circuit constructed from eight gates is shown in Figure 5.7. The latch can be built with eight cuboid gate cells (Figure 5.8(b)). Within the framework of the layout model this three-dimensional layout is optimal, in the sense that the connectivity of the circuit is satisfied by abutment of the eight active cells alone. Note that in two-dimensions, the layout requires an additional three wiring cells

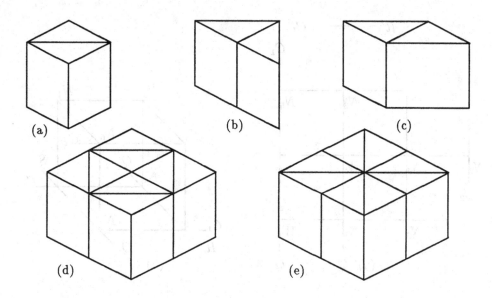

Figure 5.6: Right-angle triangle prism tessellations

W to complete the circuit (Figure 5.8(a)). It must be remembered, however, that the two-dimensional cell is smaller than the three-dimensional cell with the same functionality, though only by the area required for vertical vias and by the additional wiring possibilities introduced by such vias.

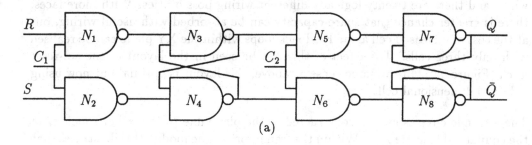

Figure 5.7: A set-reset latch circuit

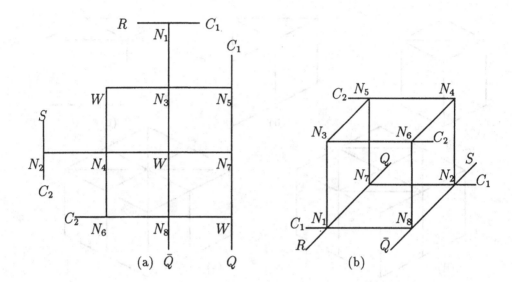

Figure 5.8: Two- and three-dimensional layouts of a set-reset latch

5.3.4   Hexagon based prisms

There is a degree of duality between the equilateral triangle based and the hexagon based prisms. The grid-equivalent of one type of prism inscribes prisms of the other type. With eight faces, the passive cell is capable of routing four electrically distinct wires, and there are twenty logically different wiring possibilities. With more faces, there is greater chance that spare capacity can be absorbed with useful wiring, but at the cost of increased cell area. Feedback loops within the XY plane can be realised with only three cells. The effect of this can be seen in the layout of the set-reset latch (Figure 5.9). In the same sense as above, this layout is optimal but now using only two-dimensional cells.

These simple circuits can be constructed in the plane due to the richer topology of the equilateral triangle grid. Within the framework of the model, this illustrates that small, isolated pieces of circuitry do not in themselves need the three-dimensional juxtaposition of nodes for efficient layout. However, larger circuits have greater connection requirements in terms of signal fan-out and global wiring. Unfortunately, it becomes impractical to layout circuits by hand with more than around ten nodes in three-dimensional, non-orthogonal grids. Exploration of the benefits of three-dimensional circuits must be done with automated layout methods applied to non-

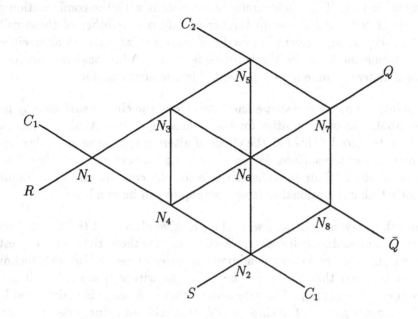

Figure 5.9: Set-reset latch constructed from hexagons

trivial circuits.

5.4 Layout methods

5.4.1 Forming abutments

The proposed method of forming layouts using abutting cells is essentially con-structive. Nodes are selectively assigned to adjacent cells and once placed cannot be removed. A signal which connects the nodes in two adjacent cells, and which is assigned to the abutting faces is likewise permanently assigned. In this way, a cluster of abutting cells is formed, presenting a surface of visible faces offering a signal interface which provides opportunities for further abutments.

When a pair of nodes has been assigned to abutting cells and a particular signal has been assigned to the abutting faces, specific configurations for those two cells are implied. Another node can then be assigned to a cell abutting either of the original cells at a visible face. This choice must be consistent with the configuration of the original pair of cells, and serves to further specify one or other of those cells. In general, the original assignment is now fixed since any attempt to alter either cell might undermine the basis for the third assignment. Additional reasons for using wholly constructive techniques are presented in the next chapter.

At some point, the particular shape and interface of the cluster surface may present no further abutment opportunities for the remaining nodes. At this point, passive cells can be introduced. This has the effect of altering the shape and relaxing some of the constraints of the surface. When all nodes have been placed, a sea of passive cells can be abutted. This provides a space for the completion of all unfinished routing, for which conventional routing techniques can be employed.

This approach to layout contrasts with the iterative placement techniques favoured in gate array and standard cell design, which proceed without the need to investigate the precise signal connections of neighbouring gates or cells. For such techniques, it is always assumed that there will be sufficient wiring space between gates or cells to complete the routing. For gate arrays, this sufficiency is maintained by not fully utilising every gate on the chip, a typical maximum being 90%. For standard cell design, the sufficiency is maintained by limiting the total area of the cells as a percentage of the available chip area, thereby allowing channels of sufficient width for the routing to be formed between rows of cells.

5.4.2   Routing space

In the abutment model, routing occurs as an integral part of the constructive placement, and the method is therefore seen as a combined placement and routing technique. In general, placements will be made to maximise the number of connections made between abutting cells. When a placement is made, there may not be a signal which can be assigned to a pair of abutting faces. For flexibility, at this juncture a routing channel can be inserted. A routing channel is simply a connection between two abutting cells to which no signal has yet been assigned. The channel may be either the continuation of an existing routing channel at the cell, or may be new. Signals can be assigned to such channels during a later routing phase. Note that in practice, the creation of such channels imposes constraints on the abutting cells. This is discussed fully in the next chapter.

Routing space in the form of passive cells can also be deliberately inserted at various stages during the placement. In this way, the abutment model can be made to create more conventional layout structures such as strips of cells separated by channels, or arrays of cells separated by a wiring grid. This is simply achieved by imposing rules which determine whether a cell may be active or passive. The rules do not necessarily need to define completely regular wiring areas. Indeed, the rules for determining how much wiring space to insert can be influenced by the preceding layout. In this way, discretionary routing space of variable size can be inserted as the need arises.

5.4.3 Relationship to other methods

For two-dimensional layout, wholly constructive placement techniques are now rare due to the inability to form good placements for large circuits and the inability to undo bad choices made early in the process. Iterative and combined constructive/iterative techniques dominate, but are still inadequate in some areas. Iteration is unable to distinguish local and global cost minimisation, and unfortunate choices can lead to far from optimal solutions. This is often avoided with repeated layout using different random seeds, which can involve considerable computational expense.

Reasons for exploring abutment as a method of layout in three-dimensional circuits have been given. As indicated above, abutment must draw on constructive layout techniques. However, the richer topology of three-dimensional layouts which offers a greater choice of relative cell positions than in two dimensions may enhance a constructive clustering approach. Nevertheless, it is still unlikely that single seeded clustering would produce consistently good layouts for a range of large circuits. The technique of abutment is likely to be of most use when applied to some subset of the nodes and signals in the whole circuit. Two broader strategies of layout which incorporate abutment are described below.

The most obvious strategy is to first partition the logic into blocks in the style of a two-dimensional floor plan. Such partitioning can be algorithmically imposed on the flat circuit description, or can be implied by the structure of the hierarchical circuit description. As discussed in chapter four, the three-dimensional equivalent of a floor plan involves partitioning into cuboids. Note that all cuboids may be constrained to be the same height, for example the maximum number of layers which the three-dimensional process will sustain. Within each cuboid, a clustering layout by abutment is used. The seed may be heuristically or randomly chosen, and the layout of each cuboid may be repeated. This is especially important when the abutment algorithms offer an indistinguishable choice of placement, which should be taken randomly.

An alternative strategy is to consider the nodes of the circuit uniformly distributed throughout the three-dimensional layout space. The positions of the nodes can be iterated to minimise some cost function. The cost function might depend upon the total distance between a node and all the connected nodes, or may include some estimate of wiring density through the space. Multiple clustering seeds can then be chosen uniformly through the space. Clustering around each seed can occur in parallel, using the positions of the unplaced nodes in the evaluation of the clustering cost function. Unplaced nodes can be reiterated periodically between clustering phases using a cost function which can now be modified to depend additionally upon the positions of those nodes which have been placed.

5.5   Extensions to the basic scheme

5.5.1   Additional connectivity

The above discussion has concentrated on layout by abutment using cells based on tessellating solids with one connection per face. It is pertinent to consider extending this model to allow more than one connection per face. This would clearly tend to increase the size of the cells by increasing the number of connection permutations which must be handled. However, it is also worthwhile to consider providing multiple connections through abutting faces of adjacent passive cells only. This is highly practical since, in general, passive cells have spare unused volume which can be used for just this purpose. Greater material utilisation is a desirable feature of this addition.

In terms of the equivalent grid, increasing the wiring capacity of groups of passive cells produces regions of finer granularity connection. This is precisely what is required to help solve the routing problem, not just in the volume of passive cells which are used for the final routing, but also for routing in embedded wiring regions created either by design or by necessity. Note that not every face need have the same number of connections. For example, the cube cell could have two connections per face in the XY plane of the transistors, but only one connection between adjacent device planes. The number and arrangement of connections in a passive cell will be determined by the chosen cell dimensions.

5.5.2 Representation of tessellating cells

The connectivity of a number of tessellating cells can be represented by the modified abutment and connectivity of a cube cell. This can be done by relaxing the number of connections per face and the manner in which the faces abut. In particular, adjacent strips of cells can be offset relative to each other. For example, consider the arrangement of cells shown in Figure 5.10(a). Each strip is offset by one half cell. Connections are considered through every overlapping face or part face. The equivalent grid is topologically the same as the grid of the hexagon based prism (Figure 5.10(b)).

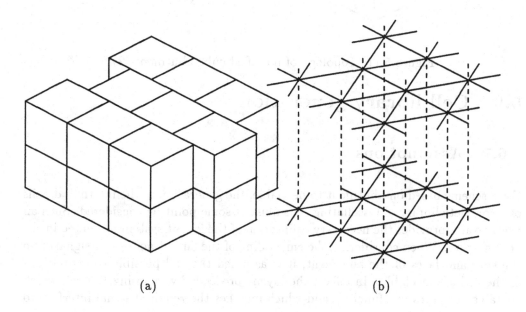

(a)   (b)

Figure 5.10: Topology of modified cube abutment (1)

Additionally, entire planes of cells can be offset relative to each other. In the arrangement shown in Figure 5.11(a) strips in each plane are offset by a half cell and cells in adjacent planes are offset by a quarter cell. If connections are considered only at partially overlapping faces, each cube is connected to twelve adjacent cubes. The grid equivalent of cells arranged in this way is topologically equivalent to the grid of the rhombic dodecahedron (Figure 5.11(b)).

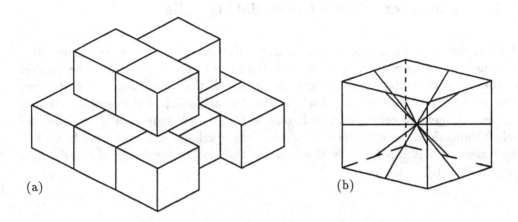

(a)   (b)

Figure 5.11: Topology of modified cube abutment (2)

5.6   Cell library generation

5.6.1   Assumptions

For a scheme based on abutment to be viable, the generation of the internal details
of a complete library of tessellating cells must at some point be considered. Such an
exercise also provides the necessary calibration of the layout system presented in the
next chapter. When considering the embedding of the circuit nodes and signals into
the cells and faces of the abutment, it is assumed that all possible configurations
of the cell are available. In effect, the layout proceeds by choosing the cell which
contains the necessary function and which matches the required signal interface to
the abutting neighbours.

As already mentioned, such cells must ultimately be constructed from planes of transistors and horizontal and vertical connections. The technology of three-dimensional
integration clearly constrains the vertical connections to be orthogonal to the planes
of transistors. However, there is greater flexibility of angles between features in the
transistor plane as with two-dimensional design. For example, angles of 135° or 120°
can be subtended without problem.

5.6.2 Cell functionality

An important consideration is the determination of the range of available logic functions in the library. Since each cell must ultimately have the same size, the simplest
passive wiring cell has the same volume as the most complex active cell. For efficiency, it is required to maximise the proportion of the volume which is actually
used in each cell. Actual cell layouts have a range of volume utilisations, and the
distribution of utilisations for given libraries of cells could be formed (Figure 5.12).
The utilisation of a cell is taken to be the volume of its bounding polyhedron expressed as a proportion of the volume of the bounding polyhedron of the largest cell.
Of the three distributions shown, (b) represents the best library, but by excluding
certain active cells, the library corresponding to distribution (c) is comparable.

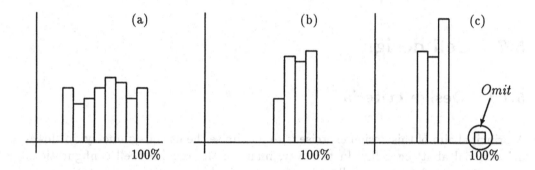

Figure 5.12: Frequency versus % area utilisation for three libraries of cells

For a particular layout, some cells in the library may remain unused. The final size
of all cells could be determined by the volume of the largest bounding polyhedron of
any cell which has been used, and the final layout of cells can be adjusted accordingly.
To avoid a wide range of volume utilisations, logic functions will tend to be simple
families of NAND or NOR gates.

5.6.3 Internal cell layout

There are two approaches to the generation of internal cell details. First, the design
of the complete range of cells could be carried out using automated layout techniques.
The input to the design problem is a specification of cell functionality, the shape of
the cell and the relative positions of the signal ports on each of the cell faces. For

active cells, it is likely that only a small number of functions with modest numbers of ports will be considered, and so exhaustive generation is possible. For passive cells, the number of incident signal ports could be greater, but now the design of the cell is a routing problem. For example, the routing between faces of a cube cell is an extension of the two-dimensional problem of routing between vertices on the sides of a rectangle, known as the switch-box routing problem.

Another approach to cell generation would be to consider the design of a smaller number of more regular cells which can be customised by the specification of internal contacts and vias. Such cells might also be transformed by rotation or reflection into the required range of cell configurations. With a small number of cells to design, hand layout and optimisation are possible. This last approach to the design of abutting cells is explored in the next section.

5.7   Cell design

5.7.1   Design criteria

A principal aim of this design exercise is to maximise the use of symmetry in three-dimensional abutting cells. In this way, many of the required cell configurations can be generated from a smaller set of basic cells by reflection and rotation. An indication of the importance of symmetry in creating an abutting cell library is given by an analysis of the possible configurations in a cell library. This was determined programmatically for a library based on cube-shaped cells. Table 5.2 shows the composition of a library based on simple NAND gates with one connection central to each face.

In the table, *Types* is the number of logically distinct types of cell. For example, a wiring cell with three distinct wires is different to a wiring cell with two distinct wires. For each type, *Groups* is the number of cells which cannot be produced by rotating or reflecting any other cell of that type. Finally, *Cells* is the complete number of cells of that type. Note that only those cells which are distinguishable are recorded. In particular, the inputs to a gate are deemed interchangeable.

Another crucial consideration is the supply of power to each cell. This requirement compromises the symmetry of cells, since a regular mesh of power and ground lines is required which must pass through every abutting cell. Random routing of power

Contents	Types	Groups	Cells
Empty	1	1	1
Wiring	10	24	202
Inverter	26	92	1712
2 Input NAND	17	81	1560
3 Input NAND	8	33	620
4 Input NAND	3	7	105
5 Input NAND	1	1	6
Library total	66	239	4206

Table 5.2: Analysis of a library of cuboid cells with one connection per face

through the cells cannot be considered since this cannot be done efficiently and would increase the number of connections to each cell. Furthermore, such wiring has special routing requirements which cannot easily be met by automated methods. In particular, power and ground tracks should only be routed in metal.

5.7.2 Design rules

The layout of three-dimensional cells must conform to some set of design rules. Three-dimensional circuits depend heavily on isolation techniques and silicon-on-insulator technology in particular. Lambda-based CMOS SOI design rules are therefore adopted as the foundation of the design rules. The rules shown in Table 5.3 are remarkably simple with 2λ predominant [Weste 85].

It is assumed that these basic design rules can be applied to additional levels of transistors. Therefore each transistor level has one metal layer. The model for vertical connectivity is simple. It is assumed that metal filled vertical vias connect any pair of adjacent transistor levels. The vias must connect metal layers in each of the transistor levels, and there must be an oversized metal overlap on each metal layer at the location of the vertical via. A double overlap of 2λ has been suggested [Mathewson 89]. The structure of the vertical connection is shown in Figure 5.13.

Mask	Feature	Rule
Island	All device spacings	3λ
	Minimum poly width	2λ
	Minimum poly to poly spacing	2λ
Poly	Minimum poly to island spacing	2λ
	Minimum poly to island edge	2λ
	Minimum poly extension over island	2λ
	Minimum metal width	2λ
Metal	Minimum metal spacing	2λ
	Minimum metal contact overlap	λ
	Distance over poly or island edge	λ
Contact	Distance from non-contacted feature	2λ
	Contact width on poly or island	2λ

Table 5.3: Lambda-based CMOS SOI design rules

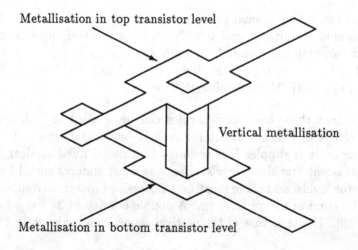

Figure 5.13: Vertical connection model

5.7.3   A layout editor

The design of a number of cells conforming to the above design rules and design criteria was explored with the aid of the Qudos Full Custom Layout Editor [Qudos 88].
The layout editor supports the manipulation of features on a number of mask layers. The number and type of layers is configurable, and so the editor can operate
on many different processes. The description of each mask layer includes rules for
feature sizes, separations and contact overlaps. Many of the rules are checked as
features are created, resulting in layout largely correct by construction. Remaining
rules are explicitly checked on completed layouts.

This system is ideally suited to the design of three-dimensional cells using the above
design rules, since the flexibility of the configuration mechanism allows vertical connections to be simply modelled with appropriately defined wiring and via layers. A
translation of the above three-dimensional CMOS SOI process design rules into the
format of the layout editor configuration file is given in appendix A.

5.7.4   Cube cells

The layout of a number of example cells in a proposed three-dimensional abutting
library is now presented. The library is based on the one outlined above and shown
in Table 5.2. Each layout presented below is drawn to the same scale, and the colour
code for the layers is given in Table 5.4.

Colour	Depicts
Blue	Metal
Pink	Polysilicon
Green	N-type diffusion
Yellow	P-type diffusion
Black	Contact between layers

Table 5.4: Layout colour codes

The overall scheme for the supply of power to one layer of cells is shown in Figure 5.14. Each cell has power and ground rails running along two opposite edges.
Alternate rows have power and ground reversed, and so the physical abutment of

cells produces alternate double thickness power and ground rails which can be simply fed from the ends of the rows.

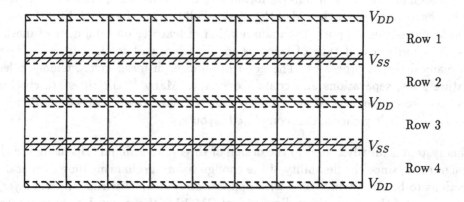

Figure 5.14: The power supply mesh of one layer of abutting cells

The layout of a five input NAND gate is shown in Plate 5.1. The vertical or Z-axis connections are located towards the centre of the cell and are marked by the oversized metal overlap. The left and right vertical connections are arbitrarily chosen to be up and down respectively. The output of the gate leaves the cell on the right but symmetry allows the output to leave on the left by reflecting the cell in the Y-axis. Furthermore, the cell can match the power rails of either type of row by reflection in the X-axis as appropriate.

A similar cell where the output leaves the cell through a vertical connection is shown in Plate 5.2. The same symmetric properties allow the output signal to leave through either the up or down connections, and to match either type of power requirement. A more complex layout is required for the output to leave the cell through the top and bottom faces (Plate 5.3). However, by leaving the power to the transistors unconnected, the cell can be reflected in the X-axis to allow the output to leave by the top or bottom. When such a cell has been placed in a row and the polarity of the top and bottom power rails is known, the power to the transistors can be connected with the trivial routing of two metal links.

The five input NAND is the most complex function in the library, and correspondingly determines the size of all cells. A passive wiring cell has many possible configurations but the most complex variation is where opposite faces connect. A cell with this arrangement is shown in figure Plate 5.4. The cell can be reflected or

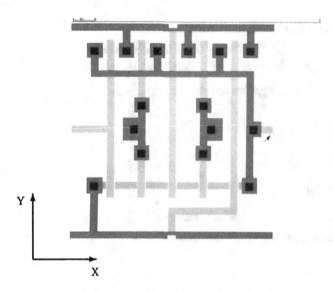

Plate 5.1: Five input NAND with X-axis output

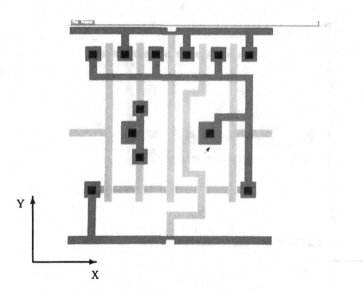

Plate 5.2: Five input NAND with Z-axis output

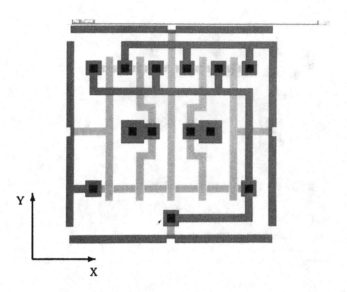

Plate 5.3: Five input NAND with Y-axis output

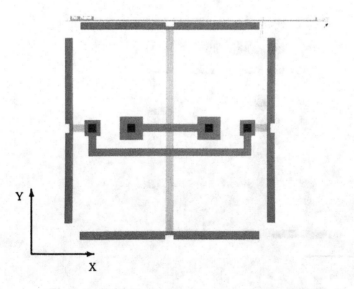

Plate 5.4: A six connection worst-case wiring cell

rotated, and the power rails feed through the final orientation with the addition of four metal links. There is scope for more wiring in such passive cells. This is discussed in chapter eight.

Each of these cell layouts occupies an area of $25\lambda \times 25\lambda$. One of the measures by which layout is judged is the length of signals as they have been embedded in the physical graph. For abutting layouts this length is entirely within the cells. Without the detailed design of all cells in a layout the exact signal lengths can not be calculated. Even with the layout of all cells, it is not clear between which points in abutting cells the length should be measured. However, on average, the length of a signal visiting a sequence of n abutting cells will be $25(n-1)\lambda$. This method of calculating distances will be used in the system of layout abutment which is described in the next chapter.

Chapter 6

Three-Dimensional Abutment System

6.1 Introduction

6.1.1 Outline

The purpose of this chapter is to present a detailed description of the design and implementation of an automated layout system based on the principle of three-dimensional cell tessellation proposed in the previous chapter. The description begins with a statement of the experimental aims and required features of the layout system and continues with details of circuit representation. This is followed by details of the design and implementation of cell and layout representation, and of the abutment algorithms. A number of important properties which abutting layouts must possess are highlighted in the details of the algorithms. Finally, the control of the abutment process is discussed through the construction of merit functions and mechanisms for combining elements of the algorithms.

6.1.2 Experimental requirements

A number of requirements of the layout system are stated at the outset. These are:

99

- Ability to specify a range of cell shapes,

- Ability to specify the connection interface,

- Flexible merit function and layout control,

- Full layout automation requiring no manual editing,

- Ability to handle circuits of non-trivial size,

- Extraction of layout data for comparison,

- A high degree of automated layout validation.

Although the cell model for abutment experiments is primarily intended to be the cube, the system is nevertheless required to be sufficiently general to be able to perform layout using one of a number of cell models. Specification of the cell model includes both the shape of the cell and the number of connections per face. An important aspect of the experiment is the determination of suitable merit functions and layout control. The run-time interpretation of the cell model helps to establish a flexible framework for the experiments.

As mentioned earlier, three-dimensional hand layout of random circuits is intractable for large circuits and for this reason full layout automation is required. A complete layout is taken to mean an embedding of the logical network in the grid equivalent at the gate and signal level. Internal cell details are not considered at this stage. The system must be capable of handling circuits of non-trivial size, say 500 gates, and of producing information by which to judge the success of layouts, for example statistics for wire lengths and materials used. Finally, since the layouts are not physically implemented, it is important to provide validation of the data structures representing layout. Self-checking is built into the system to provide validation at regular intervals in the layout process.

In the following sections, elements of layout system data structures are discussed. The first references to such elements appear in italics. The data structures are described in appendix B.

6.2 Circuit representation

6.2.1 Hardware description language

The description of the circuit is in the form of a hardware description language, similar to the HDL of the case study presented in chapter two. The hierarchic description is interpreted during the system startup. The description contains, at the lowest level, a set of leaf nodes for which no sub-structure is defined. These leaf nodes form a logical library of building blocks from which the entire circuit is constructed. As discussed earlier, the cells should be of uniform, modest area and so the logical library is restricted in functionality to families of simple logic functions. In conventional gate array and standard cell systems, there is a one-one correspondence between the leaf nodes of the logical library and the cells of the physical library. The cells are the building blocks of the layout problem.

In the abutment scheme, however, a leaf node in the logical library can correspond to many cells in the physical library. The specific match between node and cell is only determined when the connections through all of the cell faces have been assigned. At this stage, the required cell layout can be selected from a group of physical cells associated with that particular logical node, or can be constructed by customising one of a smaller number of more general universal cells.

The interpretation of the HDL results in data structures which represent the circuit. This involves the generation of unique names for the different instances of the elements of circuit description, and the representation of these elements and their relationships in appropriate data-structures. The complete hierarchic structure is preserved, though for the purposes of this experiment layout is primarily in terms of the leaf cells. However, details of common ancestry in the hierarchic structure can be used when constructing merit functions and evaluating layout order. Three elements of the data structure which represent the circuit are shown in Figure 6.1.

6.2.2 Nodes

A *node* is an instance of either a high-level or a leaf node. All nodes have three common fields, a *name*, a reference to the parent node in the circuit hierarchy, and a link to the next in a list of sibling nodes at the same level in the hierarchy and with the same parent. The high-level variant of the node represents an HDL block

```
DEF Box (In1, In2: IN; Out: IO);
    X: IO;
BEGIN
    nand := NAND2 (In1, In2, X);
    inv := INV (X, Out);
END;
```

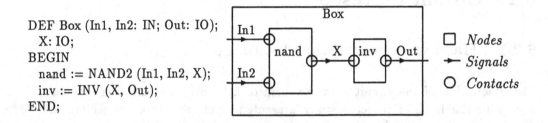

Figure 6.1: Elements of circuit representation

and additionally contains a reference to the sub-structure and a reference to a list of *signals* which are local to the block. The leaf variant of the node contains a reference to a list of *contacts* which defines the set of signals which are connected to the node. The layout process will eventually assign nodes to abutting cells of the layout.

6.2.3   Signals

A signal has fields containing a name, a reference to the node where the signal is declared, and a link to the next in a list of sibling signals declared at the same node. The primary function of a signal is to represent the connection between nodes. This is achieved through a reference to a list of contacts which defines the set of nodes which are connected to the signal. The layout process will eventually embed a signal in a set of connections through the faces of abutting cells.

6.2.4   Contacts

From the above descriptions of nodes and signals, it can be seen that a contact represents a (node, signal) pair. A *mode* field indicates the nature of the contact between signal and node, for example the signal may be an input or an output to the cell. Each contact is also an element of two lists, the list of signals to which a particular node is connected, and the list of nodes to which a particular signal is connected. The heads of these lists are in the node and signal structures respectively. The layout process will eventually assign each contact to one of the faces of the cell to which the node is assigned.

6.3 Cell representation

6.3.1 Cells

A *cell* represents the location and configuration of cells from the physical library. Cells are considered to be uniformly and orthogonally distributed through space, and a *class* field distinguishes between active and passive cells. Every cell contains two sets of coordinates, the virtual coordinate of the cell in the orthogonal space, and the real coordinate of the cell in true space. The virtual coordinate is used by rules which specify the topological connectivity of the cells, while the real coordinate is used in all calculations of distance which influence merit functions and determine wire length. The cells are stored in a three-dimensional array, indexed by virtual coordinate. This allows efficient sequential and random access to any cell. It is important that the layout algorithms are able to thread efficiently through abutting cells.

The connections through the faces of each cell are labelled with a *wire* number, and there is some arbitrary, fixed relationship between wire numbers and faces. For simplicity, the number of wires of any cell is bounded by some small constant maximum value. The connectivity between cell faces is represented in each cell by an *abutment* field, which is an array of references to other cells, and a complementary wire number within those cells. The array is indexed by wire, and so each element describes the topological relationship between the two cells which abut at the face containing that wire.

6.3.2 Rules

Rules describing the topology of tessellating cells are interpreted after the circuit structure is constructed. Specifically, the rules determine how the wires of adjacent, abutting cells match. Since cells may be geometrically asymmetric, there may be a number of possible cell *orientations* in a tessellating sequence. These orientations are enumerated by $O_1, \ldots, O_m$, and the wires from a cell to its neighbours are enumerated by $E_1, \ldots, E_n$. The integer vector $V = (x_v, y_v, z_v)$ describes the topological relationship in virtual space units, while the real vector $R = (x_r, y_r, z_r)$ describes the spatial relationship between two cells. The geometry of the tessellation is described by rules of the form:

$$(O_a, E_p) \text{ ABUTS } (O_b, E_q) \text{ AT } (x_v, y_v, z_v), (x_r, y_r, z_r)$$

The rules for cube shaped cells with one connection per face are shown in Figure 6.2.

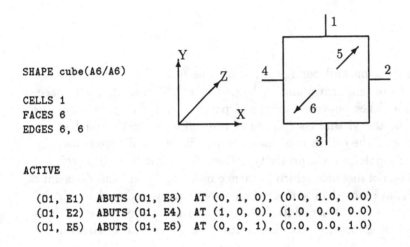

```
SHAPE cube(A6/A6)

CELLS 1
FACES 6
EDGES 6, 6


ACTIVE

  (O1, E1)  ABUTS (O1, E3)  AT (0, 1, 0), (0.0, 1.0, 0.0)
  (O1, E2)  ABUTS (O1, E4)  AT (1, 0, 0), (1.0, 0.0, 0.0)
  (O1, E5)  ABUTS (O1, E6)  AT (0, 0, 1), (0.0, 0.0, 1.0)
```

Figure 6.2: Topology rules for cube shaped cells

The capacity for passive cells to contain more than one connection per face is modelled by additional wires for which there is a further group of rules. In general, there is a single rule specifying the connectivity of each wire of each cell orientation. However, certain cell shapes, for example the right-angle triangle based prism, can have a number of possible arrangements of abutting faces. This added complexity is handled by allowing multiple rules for wires on faces which can abut in a number of ways. When an abutment is considered at such a face, one of the rules is chosen and the others discarded. The neighbouring cells must also be inspected, since rules for wires in those cells may no longer apply. Further examples of rules for a variety of cell shapes are given in appendix C.

For efficient data storage, the rules should cause a cell to exist at every coordinate in the virtual space. For a cell shape to satisfy this requirement, the grid equivalent of the face connectivity must be able to be embedded in the grid formed by inserting wires between a cell and its orthogonally and diagonally adjacent neighbours in the virtual space. Note that many of the cell shapes discussed in the previous chapter have grid equivalents which were shown to satisfy this requirement, subject to appropriate modification. Interpretation of the rules creates a table indexed by cell orientation and wire number which contains the relative coordinates of the cells adjacent at that wire. Basic consistency checks are enforced, for example, that every wire of every cell has a rule.

6.4 Layout representation

6.4.1 Clusters

As the layout progresses, cells are allocated dynamically and configured as either active or passive cells. The cell rules determine which cells may be incorporated next, and how to insert the necessary references between cells. An initial cell is allocated and designated as the layout origin, and the rules are used to incrementally build a rooted cyclic graph. As mentioned earlier, the layout employs a constructive clustering technique. With the exception of the origin, this requires that each new cell is adjacent to a cell already allocated and occupied. A convenient representation of this is to maintain two lists, one containing references to allocated and used cells, and another containing references to allocated but unused face adjacent neighbours of used cells. As each cell is used, it is moved from the unused to the used list. As yet unallocated neighbours of this cell are allocated and added to the unused list.

However, certain restrictions on the shape of the layout growth become apparent. For simplicity, it is sufficient to consider a two-dimensional orthogonal grid. Directly analogous arguments can be developed for the three-dimensional case. Consider the layout shown in Figure 6.3(a). Assume that the cells have been used in the order indicated and are all active. Furthermore, assume that the nodes in cells C_2, C_4, C_6 and C_8 each connect to four different signals. Each of these four cells must route a signal along the wire towards the unused cell C_x. Unless these four signals are electrically equivalent, or there are two pairs of two, this is an impossible situation since the routing of connections to the four nodes cannot be satisfied.

By implication, any larger enclosed space can also lead to intractable routing problems. Furthermore, the space does not need to be enclosed to cause difficulty, and Figure 6.3(b) depicts essentially the same situation. Such incongruous situations are allowable provided that any signal entering the area is guaranteed to be routed. This is difficult to arrange, and involves an earlier commitment of signals to wires than is desirable. An incongruity is allowed to form when C_7 is used if and only if one of the signals $\{A, B, C\}$ is available on the wires from cells C_5, C_4, C_3, or C_2. If this property holds, then the assignment of the signal to a wire must be at this stage before any further cells are used. If, for example, A is available at C_4, then the layout must be as in Figure 6.3(c).

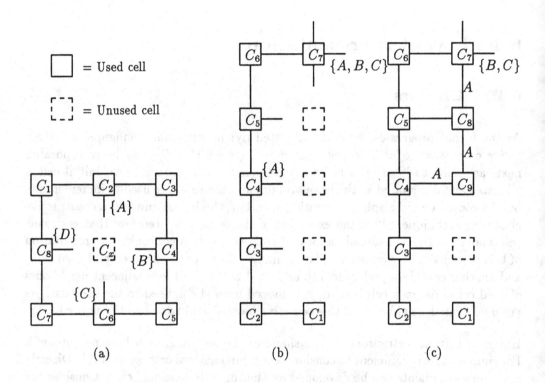

Figure 6.3: Incongruous layout patterns

In fact, this is a specific geometric example of a general problem which must be avoided by any abutment layout scheme, using cells of any shape. Signals converging along wires to an unused cell must be guaranteed an escape from that cell. A necessary condition for layout completion is for all unused cells to at all times satisfy

$$\text{Number of unused neighbours} \geq \text{Number of used neighbours}. \qquad (6.1)$$

However, this condition is not sufficient, as the layout in Figure 6.3(b) demonstrates. Each unused cell satisfies the above relation, but there is no order of cell assignment for which this property will always be true. Meaningful layout through abutment must prevent the construction of such incongruencies, and algorithms for controlling the shape of cluster growth are described below.

6.4.2 Growths

The layout process is controlled by the introduction of cell rules which explicitly specify the connectivity of cells. This satisfies part of a goal of the system, which is to develop generalised methods and algorithms to represent and manipulate layout using a number of cell shapes and connection interfaces. Control of the cluster shape is a crucial part of the layout method. However, the nature of layout incongruencies directly relates to the geometry of the cells. Unfortunately, the isolation of cluster shapes which contain incongruencies appears to defy generalised description, that is, parameterised by the cell shape. Consequently no unified algorithmic treatment of cluster growth control was found in this study.

For cuboid cells, however, incongruencies are readily identified and specific algorithms for cluster shape control can be devised. This is due to the special geometry of the cube. Growth can be controlled by imposing additional constraints on the order in which allocated cells are used. Two algorithms are presented. The first and simplest method is to use cells at a given Manhattan distance d from the origin prior to using cells at distance $d + 1$. This is easily achieved by dividing the list of allocated but unused cells A into two, A_d and A_{d+1}, distinguished by distance from the origin. As a cell is used and removed from the first list, its neighbours at $d + 1$ are added to the second list, if not already included. When the first list is empty, the lists are swapped, d is incremented and the process continues (Algorithm 6.1).

```
A_d := Origin
WHILE (nodes to be placed)
    A_d1 := NIL
    WHILE (A_d # NIL)
        choose c ∈ A_d
        use c and remove from A_d
        allocate neighbours of c and add to A_d1
    END
    A_d := A_d1
END
```

Algorithm 6.1: To force compact cluster growth

This leads to compact patterns of layout as indicated in Figure 6.4. Note that any order of cell selection from A_d will ensure a congruous layout shape. However, the concentric nature of the layout growth does impose a high degree of cell order which proves undesirable. For example, a simple inverter chain cannot be embedded in the obvious linear layout using this scheme of growth.

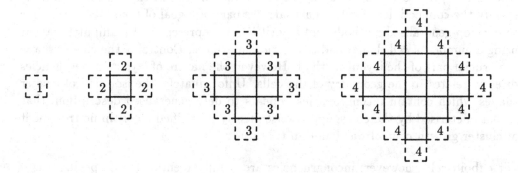

Figure 6.4: Compact cluster growth

A second, more complex algorithm introduces greater freedom in the order of cell use and consequent cluster shape. Consider the layout shown in Figure 6.5(a). Any of the unused cells is available for selection. However, if cell C_4 is used (Figure 6.5(b)), cell C_6 is no longer a candidate, and will not become one until cell C_5 is used (Figure 6.5(c)). The unused cells can be divided into mutually exclusive sets, and the selection of a cell from a set causes other cells in the set to be temporarily removed from candidacy. In addition, the selection of a cell may reintroduce candidates removed earlier.

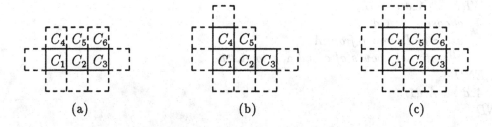

Figure 6.5: Dendral cluster growth

An implementation of this is to distinguish cells in the list of unused adjacent cells by a flag indicating candidacy for use. When a candidate cell is chosen from A, any unallocated neighbours are allocated and added to the list. Cells in the list are then checked for candidacy, based on the new updated shape of the cluster surface (Algorithm 6.2). Only those unused cells with an identical x, y or z component of the virtual coordinate need to be checked.

$A := Origin$
WHILE (nodes to be placed)
        choose $c \in A$
        use c and remove from A
        allocate neighbours of c and add to A
        check candidacy of all $c \in A$
END

Algorithm 6.2: To allow dendral cluster growth

The method for determining whether an unused cell is a candidate is as follows. An allocated unused cell $A = (x, y, z)$ is a candidate if and only if geometrically related sets of cells A_i, A_j and A_k satisfy the following conditions for all c

$$\left. \begin{array}{l} A_i = (x + c, y, z) \\ A_j = (x, y + c, z) \\ A_k = (x, y, z + c) \end{array} \right\} \quad \begin{array}{l} \text{may be used if } c = \pm 1 \\ \text{must be unused otherwise} \end{array}$$

The candidacy of A can be simply determined by enumerating the related sets and checking the used or unused status of the cells. Although initially flexible, this control scheme tends towards dendral growth. This reduces the usable proportion of the layout surface, and signal interfaces in the unusable portion of the surface are not available for connection. A higher level of control is provided by elements of merit functions described later, which positively encourage compact layout shapes.

These growth schemes for the cube are based on geometric arguments preventing the creation of incongruencies. Similar geometric arguments are not readily extended to other shapes of tessellating cell. For cells with a small number of wires, the necessary condition of Equation 6.1 may pose an inflexible order. Indeed, a growth scheme for abutting layout may only be possible by deliberately injecting passive cells at predetermined locations. For example, the order of cell use shown in Figure 6.6 requires cells at stage 4 to be passive for the layout shape to be congruous. Trial and error studies have indicated that it is possible to construct such an order, though algorithms to determine this order and the locations of necessary passive cells are not presented. Furthermore, the development of a unified method for growth control of general tessellating cells remains a challenge. The remainder of this work describes layout with cuboid cells. It is worth noting that throughout the rest of the system, no other divergence of method is required to model layout with cells of different shapes.

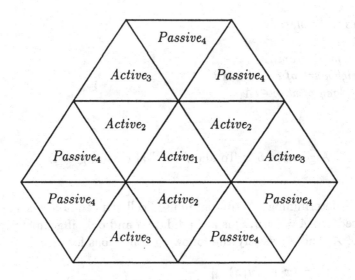

Figure 6.6: Cluster growth of equilateral-prism shaped cells

6.4.3   Ports

The presence of a signal at a cell is represented by a *port*.   Ports at the same cell are linked together, and a reference to this list is held in the cell. Ports are allocated dynamically as each cell is used to represent a passive or active cell. Such a port may be one of a number of *types*. A 'logic' port describes a signal which is connected to the node in an active cell. A 'through' port describes a signal which passes through an active or passive cell. There is a single instance of three other types of port, each allocated at system startup. These ports do not represent the presence of a signal but are used in the specification of the *interface* to a cell. There may be many references to these ports throughout the cells.

6.4.4　Interfaces

An interface is an array of references to ports, indexed by wire number, which is used to represent the allocation of signals along wires emanating from a cell. The fixed port type 'none' is used in the interface to indicate that there is no cell adjacent along a particular wire. For example, the layout space is assumed to have a planar base layer which contains the origin. For cells in this plane, the port in the interface at the wire to the lower level is of type none. The fixed port type 'free' is used in the interface at wires leading to unused cells.

When a cell is used, the free ports in the interface at wires leading to used cells are replaced by references to logic or through ports. These are created and linked to the cell, and represent the choice of signal between abutting cells. By design or through necessity, there may be no signal which can be assigned to such wires. In this case, the third fixed port type 'route' is inserted which denotes a portion of routing channel for which there is as yet no signal assignment. At some later stage, a routing process can choose to assign a signal to such channels and will replace the route port with references to appropriate logic or through ports.

A port may be referenced by more than one wire in the interface. This models the wiring of a signal across the cell. Note that the signal may incidentally connect to a node in an active cell. Conversely, ports be can allocated and linked without being referenced in the interface at all. In particular, this is true for signals which are known to exist at a cell, for example those which are connected to a node in an active cell, but which are not yet assigned to a wire. It is a feature of the layout system that the assignment of ports to wires is left until future abutments are chosen to make the most appropriate use possible of the available signals.

6.4.5　Segments

The routing of a signal between abutting cells is represented by the assignment of ports to appropriate positions in the interfaces of the two cells. Therefore, the physical path of a signal threading through the layout can be represented by lists of ports. When a signal is completely routed, there is a single list in which every port is assigned to an interface. At any previous stage there are a number of lists, representing physically disjoint portions of routing for that signal. This structure appears in each signal as a reference to a list of *segments*, where each segment contains a reference to a list of ports.

A new segment is started for a signal at each active cell containing a node to which the signal connects. As the layout progresses, ports from two or more segments may converge in the interface of an active or passive cell. At this point, the port lists of the converging segments are merged and referenced by a single segment which replaces the converging segments. Since each port contains a reference to the parent cell, a segment list describes the physical connectivity of cells and wires corresponding to the logical connectivity of signals and nodes.

6.4.6   Capacity

Each cell contains a record of its spare capacity for wiring. The capacity is the number of free ports in the interface less the number of allocated ports which have still to be assigned to a position in the interface. Furthermore, each port contains a record of its assignment state, stored as a count of the number of interface positions reserved for future occupation (R), and a count of the number of such positions currently occupied (O). These counts, together with the cell capacity are used to determine a set of possible ports which may be assigned to free wires in the interface. Figure 6.7 shows an example of three interfaces and the ports to which they refer.

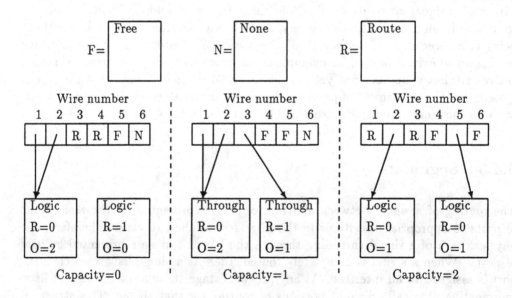

Figure 6.7: Representation of the cell interface

For used cells, the cell capacity distinguishes two cases. For cells with capacity 0, the set of ports is limited to those with R > 0, since the use of any other port will leave too few wires for the ports which are yet to be assigned. For cells with capacity 1, the set is composed of all logic or through ports. Additionally the set contains the special route port, since there is still capacity in the interface for any remaining reserved ports. For unused cells, the set contains only the free port.

6.5 Placement

6.5.1 Basic procedure

The basic placement cycle consists of choosing an unplaced node and configuring an allocated, usable cell to contain that node. This configuration may also involve the choice of a particular interface in the case where abutting used cells offer a number of possible ports. The key element of this process is the evaluation of a merit function over a search space of node, cell and interface combinations. The combination with the greatest merit is chosen as the next placement, and the layout representation is updated accordingly. The search space, merit function and update sequence are described below.

6.5.2 Search space

A search space is constructed from $N \times C \times P$, where N is some subset of all unplaced nodes, C is some subset of allocated unused cells, and P is one of a set of possible interfaces or *perms*. A perm is a specific instance of a potential interface to C formed by choosing a port from the set offered by each neighbouring cell. The perms are calculated once per cell per placement, and are formed by permuting all possible choices of ports from the contributing sets of adjacent cells. For example, consider the cell C_6 in Figure 6.8.

Cell C_1 is used, has capacity 0, and contributes ports $\{A, B\}$. Cell C_3 is also used, but has capacity 1 and so contributes ports $\{P, Q, R, route\}$. Cells C_4 and C_5 are

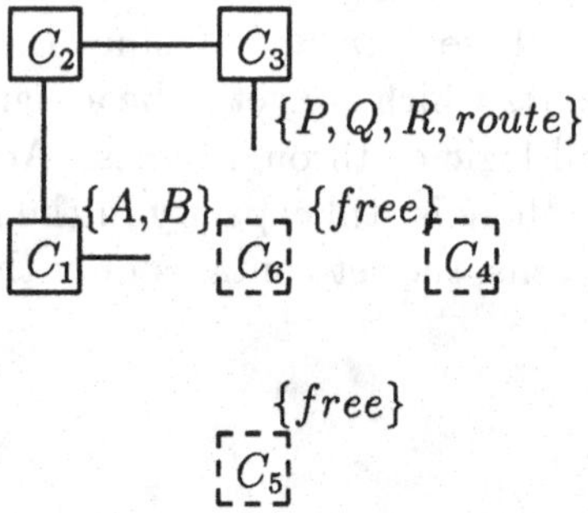

Figure 6.8: Interface permutations

unused and each contribute $\{free\}$, and so there are a total of six perms which are:

$$
\begin{bmatrix}
A, & P, & free, & free \\
A, & Q, & free, & free \\
A, & route, & free, & free \\
B, & P, & free, & free \\
B, & Q, & free, & free \\
B, & route, & free, & free
\end{bmatrix}
$$

Note that in the worst case, which offers the least choice of interface, there is a single perm. The maximum number of perms is bounded by some constant related to the number of wires for each cell. If there are w wires, then an unused cell can have at most $w/2$ used neighbours each of which can contribute at most w ports. The upper bound on the number of permutations is therefore given by $w^{w/2}$, which clearly grows quickly as w increases. However, this bound is not tight, since in practice layout combinations constrain adjacent cells to have smaller contributing sets. Note also that where two or more wires are incident from the same cell, the order of assignment of ports from the contributing set of the cell to the wires of the interface is unimportant. This significantly reduces the number of permutations for cells with more than one connection per face.

6.5.3   Merit functions

The construction of the search space has been outlined. This space is searched by evaluating a merit function for each element of the space. An element consists of a node, cell and perm triple (N, C, P). The triple yielding the maximum merit is chosen as the next placement to be made. The canonic form of the merit function M is given by

$$M(N, C, P) = Y(N, C, P) \times \sum_i W_i F_i(N, C, P) - \frac{1}{Y(N, C, P)}$$

where Y is a step function which determines if the triple is a valid placement, W_i are weights and F_i are functions which quantify some feature of merit. The step function Y is 1 (valid) if

$$\overbrace{capacity(C)}^{a} \geq \overbrace{contacts(N)}^{b} + \overbrace{non.free.ports(P)}^{c} - \overbrace{matching.signals(N, P)}^{d}$$

and 0 (invalid) otherwise. Invalid triples therefore attract a minimum merit of $-\infty$. Terms a, b and c are readily available. Term d is determined by pattern matching. As an example consider a node N which connects to signals (X, Y, Z). In Figure 6.8, all of the six triples formed by N, C_6 and the perms of C_6 are invalid. If N instead connects to (A, B, Q) then four triples are valid. Despite the node having three contacts and every perm having two non-free ports, there are two matching signals between the ports of the perm and the contacts of the node.

The weighted functions F_i quantify the benefit of choosing a particular triple according to some feature of the triple and the current state of the layout. The weights W_i are determined at run-time to explore the effect of the corresponding merit component. The components are of two types, static or dynamic. Static components are naturally bounded by some small known constant. A key static component is the number of matching signals, term d above. Since the investigation is to determine the efficacy of abutment as a placement and routing scheme, it is reasonable to suppose a high weight would be attributed to this component.

A second static component is the connectivity of the node, term b above. Provided suitable ratios are maintained between the weights, this component will roughly determine whether simple or complex nodes are used first. A third component is used to favour the choice of perms where different segments of the same signals merge. It may be beneficial to complete routing as soon as possible, to avoid having to use the capacity of cells placed later, and to keep routing paths as short as possible.

A second type of component is dynamic and grows in magnitude as the size of the layout increases. In order to avoid such components swamping the effect of the static components, they are scaled by the size of the bounding box of the current layout. Such components are principally distance related. For example, one such component is the minimum distance from unmatched signals in a proposed triple to other segments of the signals which are already positioned in the layout. This will tend to cluster related nodes in the same vicinity, once again helping reduce the amount of extra routing involved. A fuller discussion of the merit function, and the weights attributable to the various components is given in chapter seven.

6.5.4   Update sequence

Having evaluated the search space with the merit function and chosen a triple yielding the greatest merit, the assignment of cell, node and interface must be made. This involves a number of steps. First, the cell is marked as used, and removed from the unused list. The unused neighbours are added to the list if not already present, and a reference to the node is created. Second, the node is marked as placed and a reference to the cell created. Third, logic type ports are created for each contact at the node. These are linked together and referenced by the cell, the capacity of which is marked down accordingly. Fourth, the wire assignment is formed for matching segments in neighbouring cells, causing appropriate wires in the interfaces of the cells to reference the matching ports. This matching involves the merging of signal segments, since each new logic port is created with a new segment number.

6.5.5   Blockages

As discussed earlier, incongruent cluster shapes must be avoided to prevent signals becoming trapped. There is, however, another similar problem which can occur in otherwise valid cluster shapes. Consider Figure 6.9(a) where node N connecting signals (D, E, F, G) has been chosen at cell C_5. The signal D is matched along the wire between cells C_1 and C_5. In this situation, however, D has no means of escape from the pair of cells. This is allowable if D is not connected to any other node in the circuit, otherwise N is not a permissible choice at that cell. The situation is not always determined by simply inspecting pairs of cells since in the general case the whole of the space populated by segment D must be inspected (Figure 6.9(b)). The assignment indicated can be made provided D is still free to escape from the cluster via spare capacity at some other cell. For a single segment, this is easily determined and enforceable. However, several nets may be competing for the spare capacity of the same cells on the surface of the cluster.

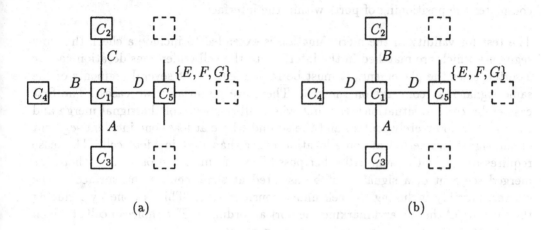

Figure 6.9: Blocked signals

Consider the complete set of segments $S = \{s_0, \ldots, s_n\}$, and the set of cells on the surface of the cluster $C_0, \ldots, C_m$. Each C_i has a (non-empty) set of available segments $\Gamma_i \subset S$, which is derived from the set of contributing ports for C_i. After every cell use, it is required that each Γ_i to be represented by a set of segments $\gamma_i \subset \Gamma_i$ such that $\bigcup \gamma_i = S$. The determination of γ_i which satisfies this property is in general computationally expensive. The problem is directly related to a well known problem in graph theory, the marriage problem, a version of which is posed as follows. Given n boys and m girls $(m > n)$, where each boy knows some p girls $(p \leq m)$, can all the boys be married such that every boy marries a girl he knows? The relationship with the above problem is seen by considering the boys as segments S, the girls as segment sets Γ, and marriage as the selection of the segment subsets γ.

The usual approach to solving the marriage problem is to utilise the min-cut max-flow optimisation method. This requires computation proportional to the square of the number of boys. The validity check of every merit function evaluation would, in effect, require the solution of the marriage problem. In view of the large search spaces which are desirable for making the best choice of placement, it is not an acceptable proposition to perform this test. Instead, a simple technique is employed which guarantees a solution and therefore obviates the need for an explicit test. As a segment is created, it is arranged to be assured an exit at some cell on the surface of the cluster. That is, the segment is guaranteed assignment to a wire by reducing the capacity of some cell and increasing the reserved count of the appropriate port. Note that the actual assignment is still deferred until the placement of abutting cells completes the positioning of ports within the interface.

The test for validity in the merit function is extended to include a check that any segments which are matched in the interface to the cell under consideration can be asserted after the placement. It must be remembered that several segments of the same signal may converge on the cell. There are essentially two cases. The first case embraces two situations, the first where all segments of the signal merge and the signal is completely routed, and the second where at least one incident segment of the signal is asserted at some location other than that incident cell. This case requires no explicit action. All other possibilities form the second case, where the merged segment of a signal must be asserted at some cell on the surface of the cluster, possibly including the cell under consideration. This is done by reducing the capacity of the cell and marking the port accordingly. The choice of cell at which a segment is asserted is discussed in the next chapter.

6.6   Routing

6.6.1   Routing space

Each (node, cell, perm) triple chosen from the search space may contain route ports in the interface of the perm where connection is not possible and the cell has spare capacity. As the layout extends, further route ports may be added forming a routing channel of arbitrary size and shape. This channel, created as a by-product of the placement process, is used as a starting point for completing the routing not achieved by direct abutment. For example, consider the layout of Figure 6.10. The route ports between cells C_3, C_4 and C_5, inserted when these cells were used, create a channel through which it is possible to route the segments A_1, A_2, A_3 of signal A. Routing channels are free to be used in any way, since route ports are only allocated to an interface when a cell has spare capacity, and are never required to satisfy any of the assertion requirements of segments.

There will come a point in the placement process where no node can be placed in any of the available unused cells with any of the available interfaces. This may be because there are no nodes to place or, at some earlier stage, because none of the combinations in the search space are valid. In such circumstances, the routing space can be augmented as necessary by the placement of a selection of passive cells on the cluster surface. Where the contributing sets of adjacent cells permit, the allocation of such passive cells automatically causes route ports to be selected. Indeed, when all placement is done, surface layers of passive cells can be added to boost the channels which define the routing space. The layout process can therefore be seen as a combination of placing active and passive cells.

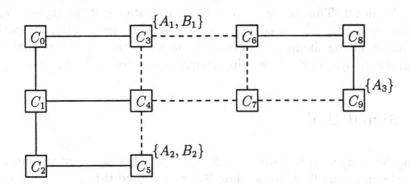

Figure 6.10: A simple routing channel

6.6.2   Basic procedure

The routing problem can be stated as follows. Consider the routing space formed by route ports in the interfaces of adjacent cells $C_0, \ldots, C_r$. Note that there may be a number of disjoint routing spaces. At each cell C_i there is a set of all the available segments $\gamma_{(i,0)}, \ldots, \gamma_{(i,s)}$. It is required to find two sets of cells R_a and R_b threading through the routing space such that $R_a \cap R_b \neq \emptyset$, and $\gamma_{(a,i)}$ and $\gamma_{(b,j)}$ are two segments of the same signal, for some $C_a \in R_a, C_b \in R_b$. There is then a path of route ports from C_a to C_b which can be replaced by ports referring to segments $\gamma_{(a,i)}$ and $\gamma_{(b,j)}$. Furthermore, these segments will meet in the interface of some cell, and will be merged. If $\gamma_{(a,i)}$ and $\gamma_{(b,j)}$ are the last two remaining segments the signal is completely routed.

One of the simplest area routing algorithms is due to Lee [Lee 61]. In the usual two-dimensional case it is often described to behave in terms of a spreading ink blot. An ink drop represents the seed signal, and the blot spreads in all directions until one of the signal counterparts is reached. At this point, the path traced is claimed, and the process repeats from this new initial state. In fact, to route a signal using the minimum distance, it is necessary to use an ink blot for each instance of a signal segment and spread concurrently from each source. Consider the channel shown in Figure 6.10. If C_9 is arbitrarily chosen as the single seed, then the blot will reach C_3, perhaps through C_6, distance 3. The minimum distance between C_5 and any other cell containing a segment of A is 2 and so the total distance to complete the routing of A is 5. However, if seeds C_3, C_5 and C_9 are used concurrently, the first path found is C_3C_5, distance 2. This causes C_4 to contain an instance of the signal. When the second blot proceeds, using seeds C_3, C_4, C_5 and C_9 concurrently, the path C_4C_9 will be chosen, giving the minimum possible path length of 4. This simple routing algorithm is employed in the three-dimensional space created by the route channels.

6.6.3   Signal choice

There may be many ways to route a number of signals through a given routing space. For example, in Figure 6.10, signal A or B can be routed through C_4, but not both. In general, a given section of routing channel may be capable of fulfilling the routing of a number of mutually exclusive sets of signals. As the space grows, the number of sets of signals which can be routed increases. A simple heuristic approach to channel utilisation can be formed. For example, if a signal can be fully routed using the channel, then this may be a desirable goal, and can take precedence over other uses of the channel. Another goal might be to use as much of the channel as possible. However, since the channel can always be extended and therefore does not represent a fixed space as found in, say, gate array layout, this may be less important.

For a given route channel and set of signals which are available in that channel, a routing merit function can be used to select a signal to route. As with the placement merit function, there are two components. First, a check that some routing can be done on the signal. This involves a dry run of the ink blot procedure, but without performing any lasting modification of the layout representation. Second, a simple figure of merit is calculated, based on the heuristics above. For example, a high weight can be attributed to the choice of a signal which can have all its segments merged in the routing space. A secondary element can be used to distinguish signals which are capable of being completely routed, that is, when all nodes to which the signal connects have been placed. Once the choice is made, the route proper is conducted. The assignment of wires is performed by replacing route ports by ports of type through. There is no requirement to assert any signal so routed, since this is achieved independently during the placement of cells.

6.7 Control and validation

6.7.1 Layout control

The placement process is defined to be some combination of placing a node, inserting routing space by placing passive cells, and routing. These operations can clearly be interleaved in many ways. For example, it might be beneficial to forge ahead and do all the placement possible before inserting routing space. An alternative strategy would be to integrate small amounts of routing space at regular intervals in the placement. To allow the investigation of a number of layout policies, an interactive method of algorithm control was implemented. Three primitives `place`, `space` and `route` are the algorithmic building blocks. Two further primitives allow the specification of search spaces, `consider` (to choose a set of nodes) and `include` (to choose a set of frontier cells). Groups of commands are built recursively from these primitives. A `repetition` clause iterates a group.

For example, a complete sequence to fully layout a small circuit might be:

```
1  repeat forever
2     consider all nodes
3     include all cells
4     place all nodes
5     space all surface
6     route all signals
7  end
```

Commands 1 and 7 delimit a group which will be repeated until all nodes are placed and all signals are fully routed, or until an error condition is raised. Commands 2 and 3 define the scope of the search space for the placement/routing exploration. Since the circuit is small, the full search space can be enumerated. Command 4 repeatedly explores all unplaced nodes in all unused candidate cells with all possible incident perms. This rule terminates when there are no more nodes to place, or no node will fit in any of the available cells with any of the available perms. Rule 5 extends the current route space by using up the remainder of the current surface. Finally, rule 6 proceeds to explore the whole routing space considering all possible signals and routing the one chosen by the merit function. This rule is repeated until no more signals can be routed in what remains of the routing space.

6.7.2   Layout validation

Since the layout is not physically validated by construction, it is important to include consistency checks in the layout representation at various stages during the application of the algorithms. Without such checks, errors and inconsistencies can remain undetected. This can lead to falsely optimistic or pessimistic results. Each of the major types of object in the layout data structures has a validation procedure, designed to operate when the layout is in a stable state, that is after each `place`, `space` or `route`. Once again, the process of layout validation is under interactive control, and a `check` primitive can be freely added to the groups.

These checks are particularly important where there are dependencies between data in different objects, and where assumptions about the state of the representation are crucial to the correct operation of the algorithms. For example, the state of each port at a cell can be used as a check on the value of cell capacity. Furthermore, the list of ports which represents a segment must exhibit the required guarantee property at precisely one cell. Such validation offers some demonstration that the layout system is manipulating objects in a sensible manner.

6.7.3   Process control

The computing environment for the circuit layout was a bank of some dozen or so DEC MicroVax processors. Process management tools were devised to automate the launch of the layout system on machines selected from the processor bank. A database of circuits and experimental parameters was created, which provided the information required by the process control system to systematically generate sequences of circuit layout processes, including repetitions with different random number seeds.

Another feature of process management was the automated scheduling of processes amongst lightly loaded machines at off-peak times. The additional information required for this was an estimate of the time required for the layout of each circuit. Furthermore, patterns of overnight and weekend processor bank machine use were taken into account. This was used to avoid starting processes which would not terminate before the beginning of the next rise in processor demand, and to make the best use of otherwise idle processors. A final function of process management was to oversee the automatic extraction of data and collation of results.

Chapter 7

Abutment System Configuration

7.1 Overview

7.1.1 Aims

This chapter describes a set of preliminary layout experiments using the system of three-dimensional abutment just described. The experiments are designed to configure the system and prepare the way for the experiments described in the next chapter. Specifically, the following questions are addressed:

- What are the important components of the merit functions?

- How should the components of the merit functions be weighted?

- What are the best algorithm control strategies?

- Is the system behaving sensibly?

The system is deliberately designed to operate in a highly flexible manner, and a primary goal of this first set of experiments is to determine those settings of the system parameters which produce the best layouts according to metrics which are discussed. This involves the postulation and evaluation of merit function components to control both placement and routing. In addition, the effect of different algorithm control strategies on layout is investigated, particularly the effect of the cluster shape and routing space controls. Finally, the system is used on circuits which are known to have optimal embeddings in the three-dimensional framework, and the results are used to indicate that the system exhibits appropriate behaviour and that the chosen system parameters are suitable.

7.1.2   Methods

The general experimental method used to determine the effect of some parameter or algorithm control is now described. First, a set of circuits for which layouts are constructed is defined. A variety of mainly random logic circuits is chosen in order to measure the layout system behaviour for a range of circuits. Each circuit is described in terms of simple NAND gates. The type of a circuit can be quantified by properties such as the circuit size in terms of nodes or signals, the average number of signals connected to a node and the average number of nodes connected to a signal. For the configuration exercise, a set of 20 circuits is used with a range of sizes up to around 200 nodes. Details of the circuits are given in appendix D.1.

For each parameter or control strategy under exploration, a sequence of layouts of the set of circuits is performed. Each member of the sequence corresponds to a different value of the parameter or control strategy. A small number of elements of the layout algorithms involve choice. The most obvious case of this is when a number of prospective placements yield the same maximum merit. An analogous case exists in the routing phase when a number of signals may yield the same maximum routing merit. In these cases a choice is made randomly, and each layout is repeated a number of times with different sequences of random choices. Another element of choice occurs when a signal segment must be guaranteed an exit at some cell on the surface of the cluster. Initially, the choice of exit cell is also made randomly.

7.1.3   Metrics

A number of types of data are extracted from layouts. These are the basis for quantifying all aspects of three-dimensional layout using the abutment scheme. The principal type of data is a distribution of the frequencies of signal lengths in a layout. Note that all measurements of signal length extracted from a layout are in terms of the size of the cell. Although this is not strictly necessary for the comparative analysis of this chapter, it is used in the next chapter to make absolute comparisons between layouts using different sizes of cell and with conventional two-dimensional layouts. Signal length is a particularly pertinent measure of layout quality, since in many layouts and for many technologies, wiring space dominates delays and contributes significantly to the total volume of materials.

Another type of data extracted is a distribution of average signal length and frequency by connectivity, measured in terms of nodes per signal. For each layout, both distributions are extracted twice, first when all the nodes have been placed and again when all the routing has been done. This provides the information necessary to gauge the quantity and type of connection achieved in the course of active cell abutment, in addition to the information for the complete layout process. For a chosen circuit these distributions can be shown graphically in histogram form.

For each circuit in the set, an aggregate of one of the distributions can be formed and a graph showing aggregate values against some circuit property such as number of nodes or signals can be plotted. In particular, a graph of total signal length versus number of nodes is a useful measure of how the layout system behaves across a spectrum of circuit sizes *for specific settings of system parameters.* However, since the topology of a circuit is not quantified by a single circuit attribute such as number of nodes, it is not possible to draw simple curves through the points on such graphs since, in general, different types of circuit with the same number of nodes can have a range of layout sizes. The data from a small number of experimental sequences can be shown superimposed on the same graph.

7.2 Merit functions

7.2.1 Assumptions

For each new component which is postulated to have some effect on layout, the system is modified to incorporate the weighted contribution of the component in the calculation of the merit function. The weights of each component are defined interactively. The merit function can have many components, and determining the best set of weights is, in general, the same as the problem of maximising a function of many variables. This is potentially difficult, requiring an exhaustive empirical search of the full problem space. Furthermore, a number of distinct sets of weights may produce similar results.

However, the problem is greatly simplified if the effect of each component is assumed to be independent. In this case, it is sufficient to maximise each dimension of the problem space separately. The values of the component weights for which the combined function is a maximum are simply those which maximise the individual functions. The independence of merit function components is assumed below. Fortunately, this broad assumption is justified by simple nature of the findings.

For the purposes of this section, it is assumed that the system is configured to perform layout using cuboid cells with one connection per face, and with vertical separation between layers of cells equal to the planar dimensions of the cell. For the example cell designs presented in chapter five this is 25λ. The total space available for circuit layout is assumed to be a box of 25×25 active cells on each of 3 layers, with a further 3 layers of passive cells to complete the routing. Furthermore, it is assumed that the dendral cluster growth control scheme is in operation.

7.2.2   Connection merit

The principal technique incorporated into the placement merit function is to favour the choice of those placements which make connection between the node and the neighbours of the cell to which the node is assigned. The results of an experiment to determine the effect of this component are shown in Figure 7.1. Layouts of each circuit were formed for two separate weights of the connection component. For both values of the weight, each layout was repeated 30 times to show the effect of random variation. In Figure 7.1(a), the component is zero weighted. This results in essentially random placement since candidates are indistinguishable and so the method of random choices described above is in permanent operation.

In Figure 7.1(b) the component is given an arbitrary positive weight, thereby encouraging placements where connections are made. As expected, removing much of the random choice from the placement process results in smaller mean and variance in the total signal length of repeated layouts of each circuit. Note that the variances are smaller in relation to the means as well as in absolute terms. To reiterate, connection weighting not only produces better layouts but produces them more predictably. The improvement in circuit layout is emphasised by the graphs of Figure 7.2, which indicate five-fold improvement.

Figure 7.2(b) shows the mean total signal length for the repeated layout of each circuit in the two cases. The 'best fit' curves are drawn using least-squares approximation and cubic spline interpolation based on the complete set of data points. The cases can be compared by normalising the means of the connection weighted

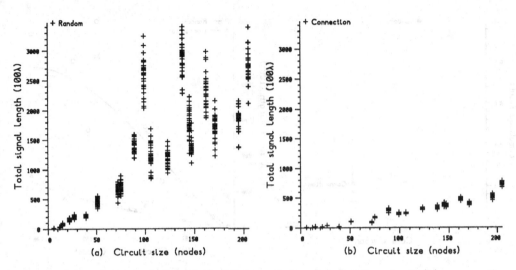

Figure 7.1: Variance in total signal length for (a) random and (b) connection weighted circuit layout

case by the corresponding means in the random case. This produces a variable of the normalised mean across the range of circuits. Figure 7.2(a) shows the mean of this variable. An error bar indicates 1.65 standard deviations above and below the mean. For a normally distributed variable 90% of the population would be expected to lie within this range.

With connection weighting, some of the remaining variance in layout is attributable to the choice of random seed for the cluster process. Note that this choice is simply a special case of the general random choice mechanism between triples yielding the same merit, since there is no context for the initial placement. Furthermore, from the graph of Figure 7.1(b), this variance is seen to be quite small. This implies that whatever the choice of random seed, the system produces layouts with similar total signal length. Unless otherwise stated, all data points shown in graphs presented in the rest of this dissertation represent the mean of the results from layouts differing only in their random choices. This is for purposes of graphical clarity, and to facilitate the large numbers of different experiments which in sum make large computational demands.

It is possible to distinguish between connections which are outputs from or inputs to the node by weighting two connection counts separately ('CO' and 'CI' respectively). The effect of various settings of these two weights is shown in Figure 7.3. The

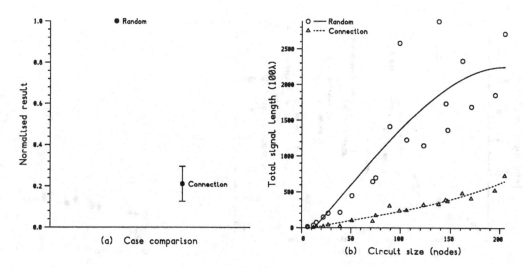

Figure 7.2: Effect of connection weighting

magnitude of the weights is arbitrary since with no other merit function components only the ratio of the weights is relevant. There appear to be three distinct groups of circuit layout. The best is where both input and output merit have the same weight, case 'CO=1000,CI=1000'. A second group of worse layouts is where the input weight exceeds the output weight. The third group of even worse layouts is where the output weight exceeds the input weight. In short, choosing placements which make one type of connection in preference to the other results in worse layout than with unstratified connection weighting. A connection weight of 1000 is assumed in the rest of this dissertation.

7.2.3   Node connectivity

A second component of the placement merit function is introduced to investigate the effect of choosing placements based on the number of signals to which a node is connected. Again, the component can be divided into two, allowing a distinction to be made between the number of connections which are outputs from or inputs to a node ('NO' and 'NI' respectively). Note that this component was introduced in addition to the connection merit. By using positive and negative weights, the function can be configured to prefer nodes with large or small numbers of signals respectively.

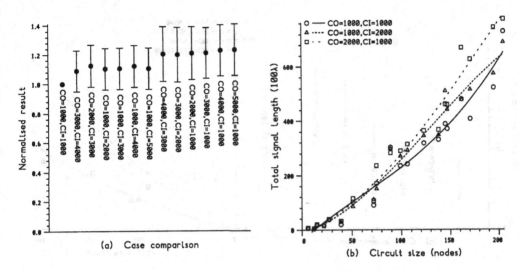

Figure 7.3: Effect of input/output connection weighting

Figure 7.4(a) shows a small negative or positive output weight ('NO=-1,NI=0' and 'NO=1,NI=0') to be little different to the unweighted reference case 'NO=0,NI=0'. This is expected, since the cell library is based on simple combinational gates which have a single output. Consequently the merit function cannot distinguish between nodes and so the weight has no effect. The case of the input weight, however, is more complex. Since there is a variety of different numbers of inputs to nodes, the value of the weight now controls a real choice. When the input weight is small compared with the connection merit weight, the layout is worse. When the input weight becomes large, the layout becomes much worse. This is because the merit function now chooses placements involving nodes with a large number of connections in preference to placements involving nodes of whatever size which actually form connections in the abutment. Note that since the cluster shape constrains unused cuboid cells to have at most three used neighbours, most nodes have the potential to attract the maximum connection merit. This component of merit is not adopted.

7.2.4 Merging signals

The layout system normally requires an incident signal to connect to the node in a prospective placement. As discussed earlier, there is rather more flexibility than

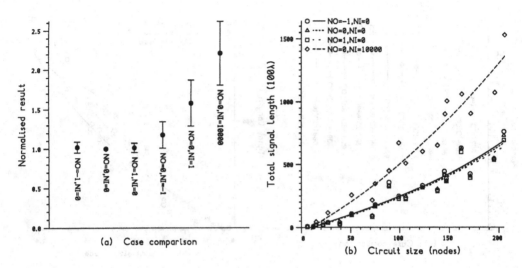

Figure 7.4: Effect of node connectivity weighting

this, since an adjacent cell may additionally contribute a route port, provided there is sufficient capacity at that cell. The test for the viability of a prospective placement can be further relaxed by allowing two or more segments of some signal to be merged *over the cell* without connecting to the node. The value of this technique can be investigated by weighting a count of the number of such merges which would be made in a prospective placement. The effect of such a weight ('M')is shown in Figure 7.5.

It is interesting that this merit function component does not appear to make any significant improvement over the standard connection weighted merit ('M=0'). This is perhaps surprising, since encouraging routing over the cell would seem to be desirable. The situation can be explained by considering the standard scheme where route ports are used if signals do not connect to the node. If there is a signal which can be routed over the cell, then a future routing phase is likely to allocate the signal to these route ports with the same net result. In short, the merge component distinguishes between immediate and delayed one-hop routing. The two approaches yield broadly similar results. The case of 'M=10000' favours over the cell routing rather than making placements where the node connects to the neighbours, which appears to be a worse strategy. This component of merit is not adopted.

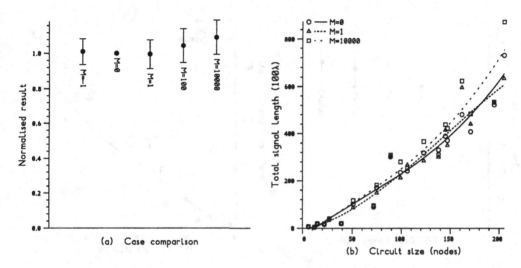

Figure 7.5: Effect of encouraging over the cell wiring

7.2.5 Cluster shaping

As discussed earlier, the dendral scheme of cluster growth is so named because of the tendency to produce spurs of cells radiating from the centre of the cluster. A component of the merit function is introduced to control the shape of such clusters. The component involves calculating the Cartesian distance of the proposed placement from the current centre of gravity of the cluster. By attaching a suitably high weight to this component, the cluster can be made more compact at the expense of aiming to form the maximum number of connections. Note that the distance is normalised by the current size of the cluster in order to make the contribution of the component to the merit function constant. Figure 7.6 shows the effect of this weight ('c').

Again, the component has no observable benefit. A more regular cluster shape requires larger numbers of passive wiring cells to be introduced since the fact that the cluster would not normally assume a compact shape implies that there are no placements suitable for the areas between the dendra. In all cases, the signal lengths of physical paths are extracted from layouts. Therefore the results of dendral and more compact growth can be compared. This component of merit is not adopted.

Dendral layout may offer the least total signal length. The same is not true, however,

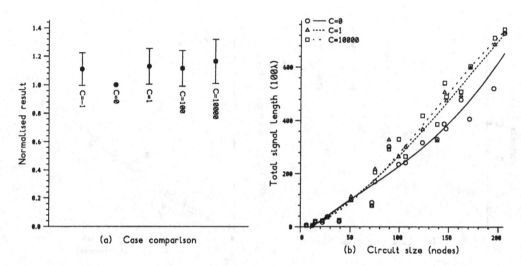

Figure 7.6: Effect of cluster shaping

for efficient use of materials. This is because physical construction requires planes of semiconductor and wiring material at least as large as the bounding dimensions of the layout. The conventional method of ensuring this in two dimensions is to perform layout within the limits of a bounding rectangle of pre-determined size. Alternative methods for abutting layouts are discussed later.

7.2.6   Cluster binding

In an experiment to control the way in which the cluster grows, a component is introduced to relate the order in which nodes are used to the number of references made to a node from within the cluster. In the first instance, references are defined by the logical fan-in and fan-out of nodes. For example, an unplaced node which logically connects to five other nodes of which three are already placed would have a binding of three. The results of various weightings of this binding ('B') are shown in Figure 7.7.

The component offers no improved heuristic for layout. Indeed, with sufficiently large weight, the results are spectacularly worse as shown in the case 'B=10000'. The fact that a node has many relations already placed does not mean that the signals between the node and its relations are available at any unused cell to which

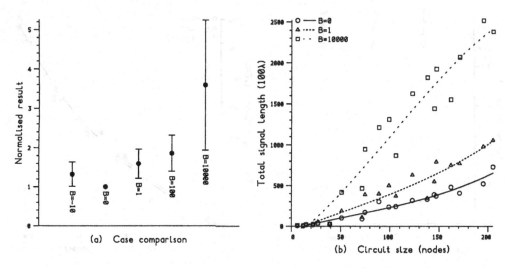

Figure 7.7: Effect of cluster binding

the node can be assigned. Other variations of this component were investigated. For example, the definition of reference was extended to include second level relations, that is, nodes which are connected to nodes which are connected to nodes. The results were broadly similar, with no improvement in layout being found. These components of merit are not adopted.

7.2.7   Segment guarantees

Another possible area of choice in the placement process was mentioned in chapter six. Segments of signals are required to be guaranteed to leave the cluster at all times. This situation occurs naturally in many cases. However, some placements require that this guarantee is renewed for certain participating segments. In the above experiments, the choice of location on the cluster surface at which such guarantees are made was random. An alternative strategy would be to renew guarantees preferentially at cells with high or low capacity. Figure 7.8 shows the effect of weighting guarantee location based on the cell capacity.

It can be seen that there is little difference between choosing to guarantee at low capacity 'G=-1', high capacity 'G=1' and randomly 'G=0'. This was not expected, since to maintain the greatest flexibility for the longest time it was thought preferable

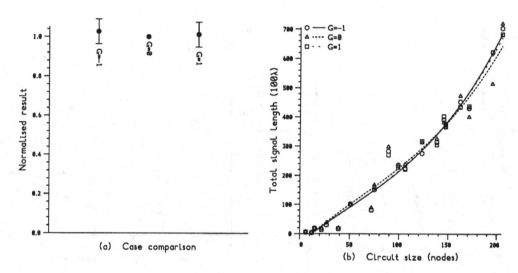

Figure 7.8: Effect of choosing segment guarantee location

to guarantee at high capacity cells. This is because guarantees made at cells with unit capacity can lead to a reduction in the signal contribution sets which those cells offer to their unused neighbours. This component of merit is not adopted.

7.2.8 Routing

The final experiment in the merit function determination phase is directed at the routing merit. Since routing is performed using a very simple ink-blot algorithm, one of the few controls over the routing process is the choice of the order in which signals are routed. Determining the length of the resulting route of a signal requires the full routing procedure to be exercised. One way of differentiating candidate signals is to check the total length of the signal which would result from the route. Figure 7.9 shows the effect of the weight ('s'). Both positive and negative weighting is shown, preferring to route long or short signals respectively.

It is again interesting to note that this heuristic does not improve on the essentially random choice 's=0'. An alternative in which the calculated length is that of the additional routing portion can be used to differentiate between using routing channels for a small number of long routes, or a larger number of shorter routes. Again, there is no clear improvement in layout, nor any distinction between the positive

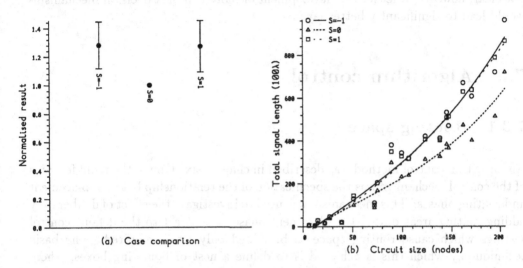

Figure 7.9: Effect of signal length preference during routing

and negative weights. These components of merit are not adopted.

7.2.9 Remarks

Some concluding remarks on merit function determination are now presented. No merit function components were found which offered any improvement in layout over the first merit function constructed. This was despite the postulation of many different possible heuristics, and the production of results from repeated layouts of a range of different circuits. This simple function is a count of the number of connections which a proposed placement makes to abutting cells in the cluster. This count is strongly linked with the fundamental mechanisms of forming sequences of abutting cells.

It is worth considering why additional components of the type investigated above do not improve layout. With the exception of the connection merit, it does not seem possible to use broad heuristics to make abutting placements which on the whole lead to better layouts. Such heuristics cannot be applied to placement in the form of a general rule which applies at all times. One way of improving layout is to make decisions based on the context provided by the preceding layout, which the simple merit components are only able to do in an implicit and limited sense. It is not clear, however, whether the development of more complex decision mechanisms would lead to significantly better layout.

7.3 Algorithm control

7.3.1 Routing space

An algorithm control method was described in chapter six. One of the main features of the control mechanism was the specification of the relationship between placement and routing phases. This mechanism was used to investigate the effect of deliberately adding routing areas during the placement phase in contrast to the default control settings which cause routing space to be added only when required. The basic technique by which this is achieved is to define a nest of bounding boxes, where each box must be completely filled before the next larger box is used. In effect, this defines concentric shells of cells which for practical purposes may be considered to be all of the same height. In the simple case, the thickness of each shell of cells is constant. Figure 7.10 shows the effect of constraining the layout to fit concentric shells of six thicknesses, measured in cell units.

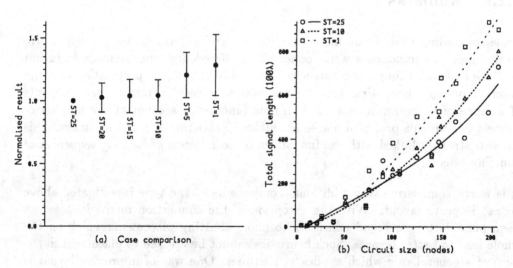

Figure 7.10: Effect of concentric shell thickness

It would appear that constraining the layout to be created in an expanding sequence of thin shells is a bad idea ('ST=1' and 'ST=5'). Note that for the size of circuits under consideration, the case 'ST=25' effectively defines a single shell which is sufficiently large to contain the complete layout. Shells must be completely filled before expanding. For thin shells, this forces some nodes to be allocated to cells where they would not otherwise be placed. In turn, this leads to the premature introduction of passive wiring cells.

By alternating between shells containing active and passive cells, routing channels can be explicitly inserted during the course of the placement. In this case, the shells for active and passive cells may be of different thicknesses. Figure 7.11 shows the effect of adding a shell composed of a single layer of routing cells between each active shell. The layouts are generally worse.

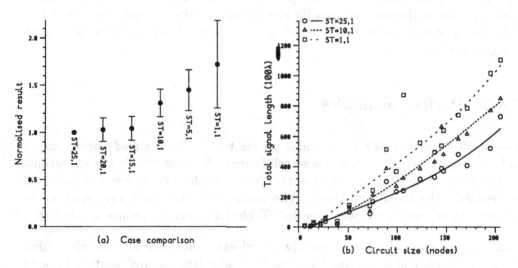

Figure 7.11: Effect of interspersing routing shells

7.4   Perfect layouts

7.4.1   Ideal behaviour

It is instructive to see how the layout system treats circuits which are known to have a perfect embedding in the three-dimensional grid-equivalent of the abutting cube cells. Within this framework, each circuit has an optimum layout, and so the actual behaviour of the system can be judged against this. This offers a degree of layout performance measurement which is independent of comparisons with other types of two- and three-dimensional layout. This novel idea of absolute layout performance is one of the features of the abutting layout system which has no parallel in more conventional forms of layout. This is because the design of cells used in conventional layout systems does not cater for the possibility of cell abutment in all dimensions. Routing space is therefore necessarily introduced, and there is no lower bound on the amount of such space which would be required for the best layout of a given circuit using those cells.

7.4.2   Perfect examples

Two small circuits, a half-adder and a set-reset latch, have already been   shown to have optimal layouts in the cuboid cell framework. Each circuit has an optimal layout of eight cells. The behaviour of the system for these circuits was investigated by repeating the layout 100 times. The number of cells which were required to complete the circuit layout was recorded. Table 7.1 shows the results of this test.

Note that the optimal layout is not always achieved automatically. For the adder, it occurs roughly half of the time. The other possible layouts involve either 10 or 12 cells, which occur roughly one third and one sixth of the time respectively. Within each group the layouts are not identical. For the set-reset latch, the perfect layout occurs roughly one quarter of the time. However, the other possible layouts are of a more varied nature than for the adder circuit, despite the two circuits having the same size. The ability of the system to do rather better for the adder than the latch is related to the complexity of the connections in each circuit. The adder has two points of reconvergent fan-out, while the latch has four feedback loops.

Cell	Layout frequency	
count	adder	set-reset latch
8	48	27
9	0	6
10	34	21
11	0	15
12	18	20
13	0	11
Total	100	100

Table 7.1: Cell count for adder and set-reset latch circuit layout

7.4.3 Lookahead

The failure of the system to consistently produce optimal layouts was investigated by examining the topology of imperfect layouts. Note that there are still elements of random choice in the process, particularly for the choice of the cluster seed. Certain choices of seed placement lead to preferred second and third placement choices which are inconsistent with an optimal layout. For the two circuits above there are no choices of seed which make optimal layout impossible, since in the perfect layout all nodes lie in an outer plane. The optimal layout of a circuit must have more than two layers to make perfect layout impossible for the choice of some seeds.

A method was devised to investigate the future implications of making placements. As an alternative to introducing iteration, future implications can be quantified by evaluation of lookahead. The general form of lookahead involves evaluating the overall merit for a sequence of potential placements and then choosing some part of the best sequence found. For computational feasibility, such an exhaustive evaluation cannot be considered for even one level of such lookahead, which would involve pairs of placements being considered.

A quick and simple alternative form of lookahead is to consider whether the placement of a node at a cell will result in new interfaces to the adjacent unused cells which are likely to match other unplaced nodes. This is easy to evaluate, since it is sufficient to consider only those remaining unplaced nodes to which the candidate node connects. In Figure 7.12(b), node C deserves special merit if there is a D which connects to both A and C (Figure 7.12(c)). This particular argument is specific to the topology of cuboid cells.

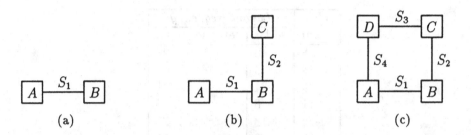

Figure 7.12: Lookahead for placement choice

Including lookahead merit causes the system to always find the perfect layout for the adder circuit. For the latch circuit, however, imperfect layouts are still generated. Nevertheless, the proportion of perfect layouts increases from around one quarter to around one half. The overall effect of introducing the lookahead component into the evaluation of the placement merit function is shown in Figure 7.13. A modest weight 'L=10' shows a real improvement over the standard reference case 'L=0'. Higher weights, however, have a detrimental effect since they encourage the placement of nodes which form good connection patterns with decreasing regard for whether the node itself forms connections. There is no point forming good connection patterns for future use if these are not then utilised. A lookahead weight of 10 is assumed in the rest of this dissertation.

7.4.4   Orthogonally connected circuits

It is instructive to consider the performance of the layout system on larger circuits which have perfect embeddings. Unfortunately, as mentioned in chapter four, the hand layout of large random circuits in three-dimensions is not practical. However, if more regular structures are considered, then the problem of hand layout is greatly simplified. Furthermore, if a notional circuit is introduced in which connections between nodes have the topology of a regular orthogonal three-dimensional grid then no hand layout is required at all, since the obvious layout of the circuit is naturally perfect in the cuboid cell framework.

The virtue of lookahead in finding the perfect layouts of such orthogonally connected circuits is indicated by Figure 7.14, which stratifies the averaged results of one hundred layout repetitions into perfect and imperfect layouts. Five orthogonally connected circuits are shown which have perfect embeddings in cubes of cells of side

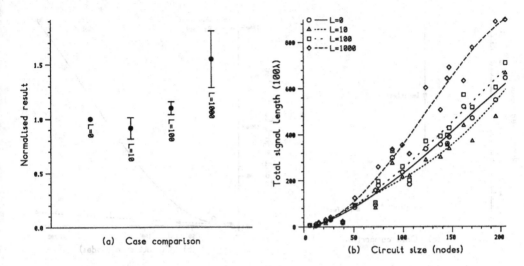

Figure 7.13: Effect of lookahead

2, 3, 4, 5 and 6. The proportion of imperfect to perfect layouts for one hundred repetitions of each of the five circuits is shown in Table 7.2. The predicted column shows the ratio of the number of internal to external nodes in the optimal layouts. Since the choice of an internal node cannot possibly result in a perfect layout, the strong correlation between observed and predicted ratios indicates that whenever an external node is randomly chosen as the seed, a perfect layout is formed. In this experiment, the allowable number of layers of active cells was increased to allow the perfect layout of the largest orthogonally connected circuit to be found.

Circuit	Nodes	Imperfect	Perfect	Ratio	Predicted
cube2	8	0	100	0.0%	0.0%
cube3	27	5	95	5.3%	3.8%
cube4	64	11	89	12.0%	14.0%
cube5	125	26	74	35.0%	27.0%
cube6	216	30	70	43.0%	42.0%

Table 7.2: Proportion of imperfect to perfect layouts

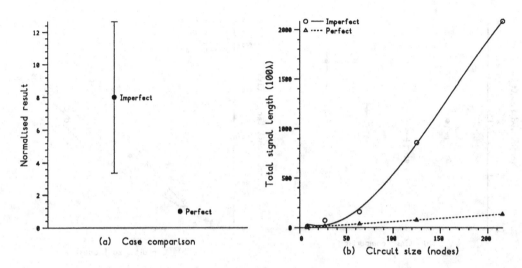

Figure 7.14: System behaviour with orthogonally connected circuits

7.4.5   Random circuits

The question of whether a large random circuit has a perfect layout is central to the purpose of the layout system. Two categories of layout perfection can be defined. Fully perfect layout describes circuit embeddings of the type outlined above. Such layouts are rare, and correspond to circuits which are either small isolated pieces of random logic or larger, more regular structures. In the many different layout experiments carried out with different random sequences, such a layout was never detected for large random circuits.

Pseudo-perfect layout describes embeddings in which every allocated cell is active at the time of the last node placement. Pseudo-perfect layout is distinguished from fully perfect layout if some signals are not fully connected at that time. Note that such pseudo-perfect layout is not uncommon, even for circuits with up to 300 nodes.

7.5   A layout example

Finally, details of the layout of a specific circuit are presented. The circuit is derived from a part of the receive logic of the CFR chip discussed in chapter two.

The detailed distributions extracted from the circuit layout are shown in the three histograms of Figure 7.15. Histogram (a) shows the frequency of signal lengths in the completed layout. Note that the lengths, which for simplicity are shown in cell units, have been arranged into 10 bins. It can be seen that the majority of signals are connected with short wiring runs.

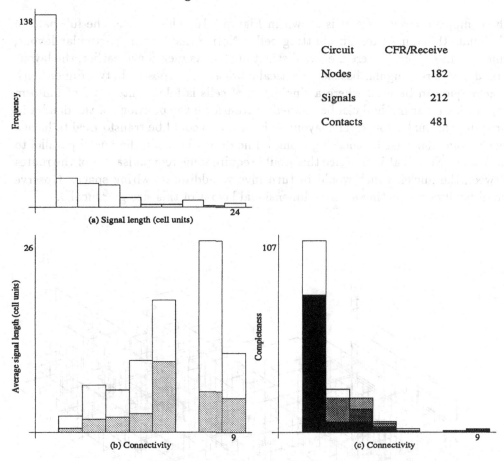

Circuit	CFR/Receive
Nodes	182
Signals	212
Contacts	481

Figure 7.15: Signal distributions from a circuit layout

There is a correlation between the length of a wiring run and the number of connections which the signal must make. This is apparent in histogram (b) which shows the average length for signals of each degree of connectivity in the circuit. The shaded areas of the bars in this histogram depict the proportion of the eventual signal length which was accomplished at the end of the placement phase. Note that this layout is pseudo-perfect. Histogram (c) shows the frequency of each degree of signal connectivity. For each bar, the differently shaded parts show the proportion and completeness of the connections which were made by the end of the placement phase. The darker the shade, the more complete the routing with black representing completely connected signals and white representing completely unconnected signals.

The completed circuit layout is shown in Figure 7.16, which traces the full path of all signals threading through abutting cells. Notice that in this particular layout, which is quite typical, there are two distinct nuclei. As mentioned earlier, the layout should have a rectangular base for practical fabrication purposes. In two-dimensions, a technique can be used where a single row of cells is folded into rows of uniform length. A similar method can be applied to transform the positions of the dendra in three-dimensional layouts. The layout in Figure 7.16 could be transformed to have a near rectangular base by shearing along a line drawn between the nuclei parallel to the Y axis. Note that in practice this would require some reorganisation of the routes between the nuclei, which would in turn involve additional wiring space. Observe the difficulty of depicting a three-dimensional layout of this size graphically.

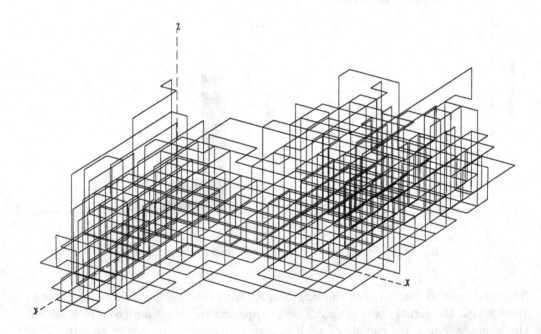

Figure 7.16: The signal paths in a three-dimensional layout

Chapter 8

Abutment System Evaluation

8.1 Introduction

8.1.1 Aims

The previous chapter presented a preliminary set of experiments which were designed to examine the performance of different operating configurations of the layout system. The experiments were confined to a single three-dimensional layout environment based on a fixed number of layers of cuboid cells with one connection per face. This chapter describes a second set of experiments which build on the above findings and which explicitly investigate the properties of three-dimensional layouts. The questions addressed are:

- How does cell library design affect layout?

- How does the separation between layers of cells affect layout?

- How many layers of cells offer improvement?

- How do the results compare with two-dimensional layout?

In the first experiment, a comparison is made between layouts using different libraries of cells. The cell design exercise presented in chapter five is revisited and the design of more complex cells with greater active connection capability is presented.

The dimensions of these cells are used to make absolute comparisons between layouts using different libraries of cells. The second experiment investigates a technological advantage of three-dimensional integration which is the potentially small separation between device layers. The effect of reduced vertical separation on the quality of layout is examined.

A key question about three-dimensional layout concerns the benefit of using more layers of active cells. This is the subject of the third experiment, which includes an examination of how the layout system behaves with a single active layer, and how additional wiring layers are utilised. Finally, two- and three-dimensional layouts are compared. The two-dimensional layout data are extracted from a standard-cell design which has been fabricated and is in quite widespread use. The three-dimensional data are extracted from layouts of the same circuit produced by a system optimally configured using the results of the experiments in this and the previous chapters.

8.1.2   Methods

The general experimental method and result presentation scheme are carried over from the previous chapter. However, an important difference is the size of the set of circuits for which layouts are formed. The set of 20 circuits used earlier is augmented with a further 20 circuits of generally larger random logic circuits with up to around 400 nodes. Details of the additional 20 circuits are given in appendix D.2. Ideally, this set would contain many more circuits. However, it must be remembered that each experiment sequence involves the automated layout of every circuit for a range of different operating conditions. Furthermore, each layout is repeated five times to sample the random variation in the system. The circuit base is therefore restricted due to the considerable computational cost of forming layouts of large circuits. This cost is discussed below.

8.1.3   Computational cost

An estimate of the computational cost of the abutment process can be derived by considering the elements of repetition in the algorithms. The primary cost of the abutment is associated with the placement phase, since this involves repeated exploration of the search space. Indeed, since much of the routing is achieved by placement alone, the time for the additional routing phase is small in comparison.

Algorithm 8.1 below indicates the stages of repetition in the general placement procedure.

```
WHILE (nodes ≠ ∅)                                        loop α
    FOR EACH (node ∈ nodes)                              loop β
        FOR EACH (cell ∈ usable cells)                   loop γ
            FOR EACH (perm ∈ perms of cell)              loop δ
                Evaluate merit (node, cell, perm)        cost ε
            END
        END
    END
    Place (best node, best cell, best perm)
END
```

Algorithm 8.1: Simplified placement algorithm

For an N node circuit, the number of repetitions R in loops α and β is simply

$$R = \sum_{i=1}^{N} i.$$

The number of repetitions in loop γ relates to the number of unused cells adjacent to the cluster. For cuboid cells, the number S of such cells for a cluster of n nodes has an upper bound given by

$$S = 5n,$$

which is the case where every used cell has the maximum number of unoccupied neighbours. Note that this case is a considerable overestimate since such cells may be the neighbours of more than one used cell, and not all are candidates in any case. The number of repetitions in loop δ is bounded by a constant relating to the number of connections per cell. For cuboid cells with a total of c connections, the upper bound E is given by

$$E = c^{c/2}.$$

As discussed in chapter six, this bound is extreme. The cost of evaluating the merit function ϵ is constant, formed from the sum of the costs of pattern matching and establishing segment guarantees. An upper bound on the total cost C_u is therefore given by

$$\begin{aligned} C_u &= RSE \\ &= \sum_{i=1}^{N} i \times 5(N-i) \times c^{c/2} \times \epsilon \end{aligned}$$

$$= K \sum_{i=1}^{N} i \times (N - i),$$

for some constant K, giving a worst case relationship

$$C_u \propto N^3.$$

Figure 8.1 shows the average time taken for the layout of each circuit. Figure 8.1(a) shows a variation in computation time even for circuits with a similar number of nodes. For a given number of nodes, this variation can only be introduced by S and E above. Figure 8.1(b) shows the base 10 logarithms of the same data. This graph has a uniform gradient of approximately 2 giving an experimentally determined cost relationship

$$C_e \propto N^2,$$

which compares favourably with the above worst case relationship.

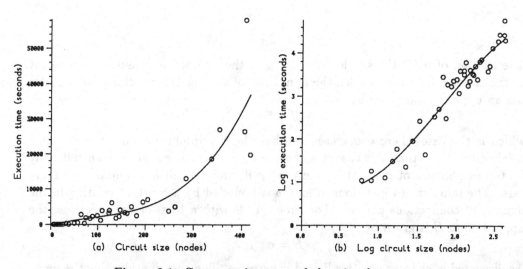

Figure 8.1: Computation cost of abutting layouts

8.2 Cell variations

8.2.1 Twelve connection cells

In chapter five, the design of cells embracing the principle of physical abutment was presented. The designs were representative of a library of cells of homogeneous connection interface and size. This library of cells will be referred to as 'A6/P6', denoting six connections to active cells, and six connections to passive cells. In chapter five, it was suggested that in the same volume, a passive cell could support more connections to adjacent passive cells. Plate 8.1 shows such a cell with two connections per face in the worst case port and wiring configuration. This configuration maps the pair of connections on each face to the pair of connections on the opposite face. Furthermore, each pair of signals is crossed over. The library of such cells will be referred to as 'A6/P12'.

A much richer connection topology is offered if active cells also support multiple connections per face. This necessarily implies larger cells since all permutations of wiring to the device and between connections must be allowed for. However, unless the functionality of the active cells is increased, additional space is required only for wiring purposes. Plate 8.2 shows the layout of a five input NAND gate cell with two connections per face. The worst case port and wiring configuration is shown. Notice the four vertical connections in the centre of the cell, which are arranged into left and right pairs where each pair contains an up and a down connection. Furthermore, over the cell wiring is well treated in this design, being mostly routed in metal.

Another example with notable layout potential is shown in Plate 8.3, in which the six connections to the five input NAND gate feed through to the opposite face. As a final example, Plate 8.4 shows a cell layout where the output of the gate leaves the cell through all spare connections. The library of such cells will be referred to as 'A12/P12'. Each of these cell layouts occupies an area of $27\lambda \times 27\lambda$. On average the length of a signal visiting a sequence of n abutting cells is $27(n-1)\lambda$. Note that despite the much more flexible connection topology compared to 'A6/P6', the average signal length has only increased by about 8%.

8.2.2 Improved layout

Figure 8.2 shows the results of circuit layout using the three libraries described above. Note that in each case, the signal lengths are extracted in units of λ, and so the results are directly comparable despite the variation in cell sizes. Adding additional connection capability between passive cells achieves around 10% improvement. Note that this improvement is principally in the layout of the larger circuits. This is because larger circuits tend to require more additional wiring space to satisfy the increased number of global connections, and so attract the greatest benefit. Recall that cells from libraries 'A6/P12' and 'A6/P6' occupy the same space.

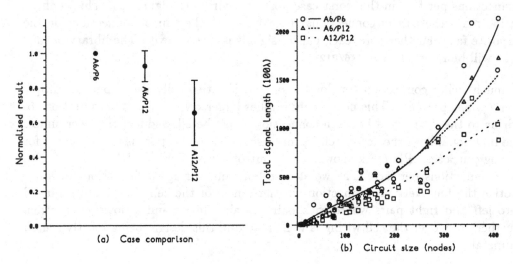

Figure 8.2: Comparison of layout with different libraries of cell

For layouts using library 'A12/P12' however, the gain is even greater, around 40%. Furthermore, the improvement is much more widespread, affecting circuits of all sizes. Note that this is despite the slightly larger cells. The simple reason for this increase in layout performance is the richer connection topology available to active cells during the placement phase. This provides the opportunity for greater numbers of signals to be routed through active cells rather than through additional passive cells. Since the cells are of comparable size but the routing is more direct, the gains are significant.

The value of even larger cells is an interesting question. Unfortunately, to form such

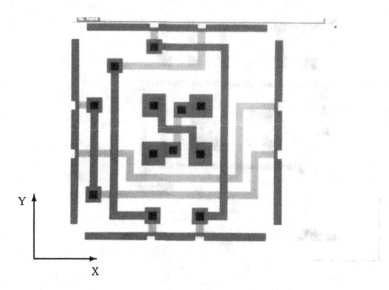

Plate 8.1: A twelve connection worst-case wiring cell

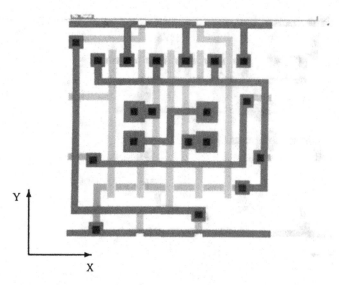

Plate 8.2: Five input NAND with two connections per face and crossed wiring

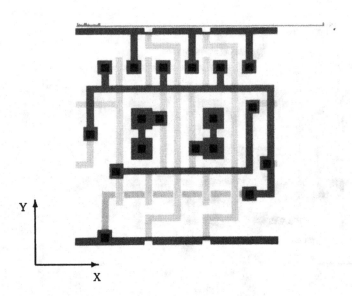

Plate 8.3: Five input NAND with two connections per face feeding through

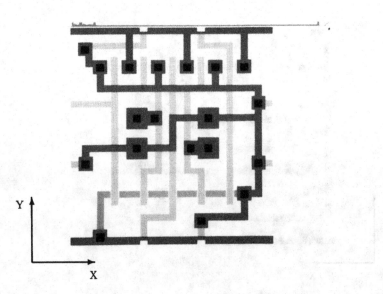

Plate 8.4: Five input NAND with two connections per face and multiple outputs

a comparison it is necessary to postulate the design of cells with the required connection interface, which rapidly becomes more difficult as the number of connections rises. Furthermore, the argument that a particular cell configuration is representative of the largest cell layout in an entire library becomes weaker. Consequently, no such design has been undertaken. However, the effect of using cells large enough to contain a flip-flop is postulated in section 8.5.5. In the intervening sections, library 'A12,P12' is assumed.

8.3   Vertical scaling

8.3.1   Scaling after layout

The circuit layouts presented so far have assumed isometric cell separations. However, as discussed in chapter four, the separation between devices in adjacent layers is potentially less than that between devices in the same layer. The problem of estimating the length of signals between abutting cells was introduced with the cell designs presented in chapter five. This problem is particularly acute for signals which enter or leave the cell through vertical connections. For such signals, there is a wide variety of signal lengths between cells. However, the vertical connections are located at the centre of the cells which gives the best possible average distance to all other connections. Furthermore, a signal routed between the up and down vertical connections has the shortest possible length, since these connections are adjacent.

The effect of assuming reduced inter-layer geometry is now considered. In the simplest case, the reduction can be applied retrospectively to finished layouts. This is easily achieved, since the lengths extracted from the circuit layouts are in fact divided into horizontal and vertical components which can be separately scaled. Figure 8.3 shows the effect of different scalings of the vertical signal length on the resulting total. Note that the scalings express the average vertical inter-cell signal length as a proportion of the average horizontal inter-cell signal length.

The uniformity of the effect is expected, and confirms that the sum vertical component of all signals is a fairly constant proportion of total signal length. From purely geometric arguments, it might be expected that around one third of all connections between cells are vertical, and so reducing the length of the vertical component by a factor of V should result in a reduction by $(V + 2)/3$ of the total signal length. In the case 'V=0.50' for example, a difference of around 10% is observed compared

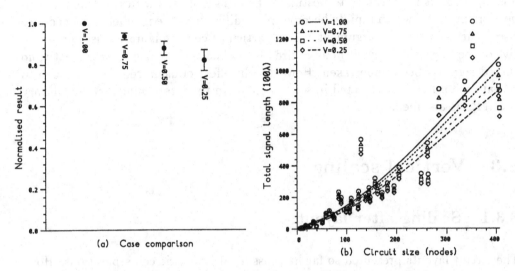

Figure 8.3: Effect of vertical scaling applied retrospectively

with the expected reduction of 17%. The discrepancy has two sources. First, cells on the bottom layer have only five adjacent cells, thereby reducing the expected ratio of vertical to horizontal connections. Second, the layout system is not capable of treating horizontal and vertical placement alike because of the constraints of the cluster shape. This introduces a degree of bias against vertical connections which is discussed later.

8.3.2   Scaling during layout

It is more interesting to consider the effect when vertical scaling is taken into account during layout. Using reduced vertical dimensions in the decision making process should result in different layout. However, the only distance related element of cost in the system is in the routing phase, during which the ink-blot method chooses the shortest available path for a given signal. Consequently, the layout differences are not expected to be great. This is supported by Figure 8.4, which shows a small improvement in each case where the vertical dimension is reduced. The improvement is uniform, indicating that the placements and resulting routing problems are little changed by the degree of the vertical scaling. The case 'V=0.50' now shows around 15% improvement.

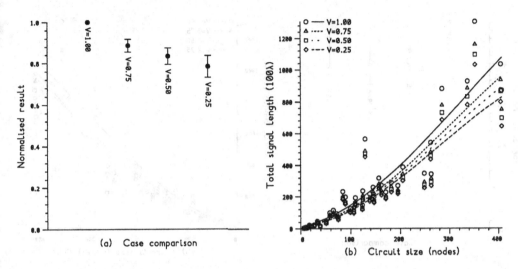

Figure 8.4: Effect of vertical scaling during routing

The nature of the layout can be more overtly affected if the notion of connection length accompanies the connection count in the placement merit function. In this way, vertical connections can be preferred to horizontal ones, resulting in different placement patterns. Since the merit function requires that better choices have higher values, the connection length component is given a negative weight to achieve this distinction. Figure 8.5 shows the effect of a negative weight on connection length. In general, the overall improvement is greater than that shown in Figure 8.4, though for many circuits there is a less clear relationship between the four layouts. The case 'V=0.50' now shows around 20% improvement, and this scaling is assumed to be in operation for all experiments described in the rest of this chapter. Note that for cuboid cells with two connections per face, this implies a vertical separation of some 13.5λ. This is a sufficient depth for the wiring, insulator and semiconductor planes in the proposed cell structure.

An interesting feature of Figure 8.5(b) is the case 'V=0.25', which overall seems to be a worse set of layouts than 'V=0.50'. The difference appears to be created by the larger circuits above 250 nodes. Indeed, for smaller circuits 'V=0.25' seems to be the best curve. A reason for this may be the very fact that reduced vertical scale is being used to encourage vertical placements instead of some more random choice. For larger circuits this tends to create poor shapes since there are only three layers of active cells and the placement begins a vertical trend which cannot be satisfied. It is expected that the problem would be diminished with a larger number of layers.

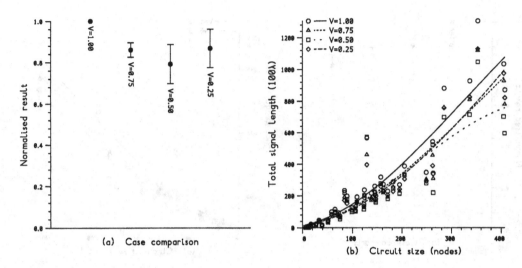

Figure 8.5: Effect of vertical scaling during placement

The relationship between vertical scaling, number of layers of active cells and circuit size is complex, and ideally the weight of the connection length should vary with each of these factors. This contribution of the number of layers of active cells to layout quality is now discussed.

8.4   How many layers?

8.4.1   Rationale

The question of how many layers of devices and wiring offer useful improvement in the quality of layout is a key question in this study of three-dimensional layout. This is because the ability to vertically stack two or more layers of devices is the very property which sets this class of circuit layouts apart from all others. Within this class, it is instructive to consider how the quality of layout is affected by the extent to which the stacking is permitted. The primary use of such information is to weigh the benefits of using more layers against the rising cost and technological difficulty of fabrication.

For all practical purposes, the number of layers of devices in any commercially manufactured circuit is likely to remain small, at least in the near future. Small implies two or perhaps three layers. However, from a more optimistic stance it is interesting to consider how layouts might change in the presence of greater numbers of layers. It is also worthwhile considering the effect of using additional wiring layers. This is a much more practical consideration but, as discussed earlier, does not offer any new connection topology to devices during the placement phase. The above discussion is now illustrated with experiments which explore layout system configurations offering different number of layers.

8.4.2   Active layers

Figure 8.6 shows the effect of varying the number of layers of active cells which are permitted for circuit layout. In each case, there are three additional layers of wiring cells. The case 'AL=1' demonstrates the behaviour of the abutment system in two-dimensions. This is discussed below when the effect of the number of wiring layers is assessed. Note that the greatest improvement occurs between this curve and 'AL=2' which delineates the boundary between two- and three-dimensional circuit layout. Using two layers of active cells instead of one leads to layout with roughly 25% less signal length.

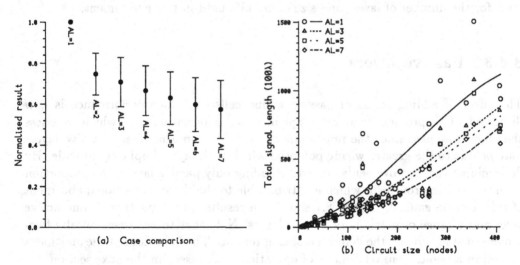

Figure 8.6: Effect of adding layers of active cells

Notice the steady overall improvement in layout as the number of layers increases. Each additional layer offers roughly a further 4% reduction in the total signal length. Smaller circuits do not show continued improvement as the number of layers increases. This is expected, and is consistent with the notion put forward in chapter four which expressed a relationship between circuit size and the maximum number of layers which can be expected to show layout improvement. For this set of circuits, the trend cannot persist since there is a number of layers beyond which even the largest circuit will not show any improvement.

A few small circuits appear to show abnormal behaviour, with layouts on a larger numbers of layers seemingly worse than those within more modest structures. A possible explanation for this is the fact that the system is unable to treat vertical growth in the same way as horizontal growth because of the geometric constraints of the cluster shape. In particular, a cell at a given XY coordinate on an upper layer can only be used when cells at the same XY coordinate on all lower layers have been used. A large number of layers in comparison to the size of the circuit can lead to isolated vertical dendra of cells which do not have the opportunity to participate in abutment. For the larger circuits, the relatively small number of layers used is not sufficient for this problem to be apparent.

In summary, a significant layout improvement is available by using just two active layers. For each additional layer there is a further more modest improvement, at least for the number of layers and size of circuits used in this experiment.

8.4.3   Passive layers

The effect of adding layers of passive wiring cells on layout performance is now discussed. This provides valuable supplementary information with which to assess the above findings, since the improvements in layout on a number of active layers may be due to the greater wiring potential which such layers implicitly provide. By determining the improvements offered by adding only passive layers, the proportion of the overall improvement which is attributable to the three-dimensional abutment of cells can be gauged. Figure 8.7 shows the results from layouts with one active layer and a range of numbers of passive layers. Note that these are essentially two-dimensional layouts by the definition of chapter one. The behaviour of the abutment system in a two-dimensional mode of operation is discussed in the next section.

Adding passive layers has a quite modest effect. In general each additional layer offers less and less improvement, and beyond 'PL=7' there is no real improvement at

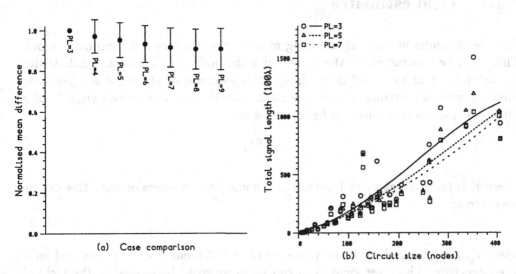

Figure 8.7: Effect of adding layers of passive cells

all. This is in marked contrast to the results for active layers, which show a sustained improvement. Furthermore, the results shown in Figure 8.6(a) and Figure 8.7(a) are normalised with respect to the same case, and so the results can be directly compared. For example, it can be seen that one active layer and nine passive layers is significantly worse than two active layers and three passive layers. It is therefore possible to conclude that for the abutment system, the gain of using a number of active layers stems from the three-dimensional juxtaposition of the cells rather than the increased wiring capability that such layers introduce.

It must be remembered that routing is achieved using a simple spreading ink-blot algorithm. However, this routing strategy produces acceptable results and is used in a uniform way for all configurations of the abutment system. As discussed in chapter two, there are more sophisticated routing approaches, particularly when the topology of the routing space is constrained in some way. Such techniques could be applied, but there is no reason to assume that the benefits would not apply equally to all system configurations.

8.4.4   Yield estimates

The above results indicate that adding more layers of active cells improves layout. This must be contrasted by the increased technological difficulty associated with the fabrication of each additional layer. An estimate of the expected yields in three-dimensional circuits is now presented. Recall that the overall yield Y of a three-dimensional structure can be modelled by

$$Y = \prod_i Y_i$$

where Y_i is the yield at mask level i. For n homogeneous layers of cells, this can be rewritten as

$$Y = \prod_c Y_{(c,n)} \tag{8.1}$$

where $Y_{(c,n)}$ is the product of the yields for the constituent masks in layer c of an n layer structure. The layer yield $Y_{(c,n)}$ can be assumed to be related to the yield of the base layer $Y_{(1,n)}$ by

$$Y_{(c,n)} = D(c)Y_{(1,n)}$$

for some function $D(c)$ representing the degradation associated with the fabrication of layer c. Substituting into equation 8.1 gives

$$\begin{aligned} Y &= \prod_c D(c)Y_{(1,n)} \\ &= Y_{(1,n)}^n \prod_c D(c). \end{aligned}$$

The overall yield therefore *decreases* exponentially as the number of active layers increases. However, it must be remembered that a Poisson modelled yield $Y_{(1,n)}$ *increases* exponentially as the area of each layer decreases with larger n.

It is useful to estimate the expected yield of three-dimensional configurations as a function of a given two-dimensional yield. This can be done by using the gamma approximation for a single layer structure of area A, and assuming that each layer of an n layer structure occupies an area no more than A/n. Furthermore, the function $D(c)$ must be specified, which leads to the postulation of a number of degradation models. In the best case, every layer of cells has the same yield, which is modelled by $D(c) = 1$. Table 8.1 shows the expected yield for different numbers of cell layers as a function of a given two-dimensional yield. The degree of observed layout improvement is included for comparison. To illustrate, consider a circuit with a two dimensional yield of 50%. If the circuit is fabricated on four layers, the estimated

Layers	Yield (%)									Layout Gain (%)
1	10	20	30	40	50	60	70	80	90	
2	3	11	21	33	44	56	68	79	90	25
3	2	8	18	30	42	55	67	79	90	29
4	1	6	16	28	41	54	67	78	90	33
5	1	5	15	27	40	53	66	78	90	37
6	0	5	14	26	40	53	66	78	90	41
7	0	4	13	26	39	53	66	78	90	45

Table 8.1: Projected three-dimensional yield, $D(c) = 1$

Layers	Yield (%)									Layout Gain (%)
1	10	20	30	40	50	60	70	80	90	
2	2	6	11	16	22	28	34	40	45	25
3	0	2	4	7	11	14	17	20	22	29
4	0	1	2	3	5	7	8	10	11	33
5	0	0	1	2	3	3	4	5	6	37
6	0	0	0	1	1	2	2	2	3	41
7	0	0	0	0	1	1	1	1	1	45

Table 8.2: Projected three-dimensional yield, $D(c) = 0.5$

Layers	Yield (%)									Layout Gain (%)
1	10	20	30	40	50	60	70	80	90	
2	1	3	5	8	11	14	17	20	25	25
3	0	0	1	1	2	2	3	3	4	29
4	0	0	0	0	0	0	0	0	0	33
5	0	0	0	0	0	0	0	0	0	37
6	0	0	0	0	0	0	0	0	0	41
7	0	0	0	0	0	0	0	0	0	45

Table 8.3: Projected three-dimensional yield, $D(c) = 0.5/c$

yield falls to 41% but a 33% reduction in total signal length could be expected for an abutting layout.

Unfortunately, as discussed in chapter three the yield of the second and subsequent layers is likely to be worse than the yield for the first layer. This can be modelled by $D(c) = k$ for $c > 1$ and some positive constant $k < 1$. For example, setting $k = 0.5$ results in degradation as shown in Table 8.2. Notice how the yield now falls off much more sharply as the number of layers increases, even when there is high initial two-dimensional yield. In reality, the degradation is not constant and gets worse as the number of layers increases. A possible model for this is to assume that the degradation at layer c is inversely proportional to c, that is $D(c) = k/c$. Setting $k = 0.5$ results in vanishing yields for large numbers of layers or small starting yields, and is more in keeping with observations of present day technical achievements.

8.5   Comparison with conventional layout

8.5.1   Introduction

So far, comparisons have been made between different modes of operation of the abutment system. This has primarily involved comparisons between layouts of three-dimensional circuits. The two-dimensional performance of the system was introduced above, and the relationship between two- and three-dimensional abutting layouts was shown. In order to further judge the performance of the abutment system, it is necessary to form comparisons with conventional two-dimensional layout. By viewing the results of the abutment system in a wider context, the value of this approach to both two- and three-dimensional layout can be quantified.

Forming comparisons with conventional layout is not altogether straightforward. One of the main problems is that the abutment system has no direct counterpart in conventional two-dimensional methods. While the novelty of the method is one of the characteristics under examination, care is required when comparing dissimilar methodologies. For example, as discussed in chapter two it is unfair to compare the performances of gate array and custom layout directly without also considering the differences in design complexity, turnround time and cost. Another problem is the practical matter of extracting the same character of data from different layout systems. This is discussed below.

8.5.2 Standard cell CFR layout

The standard cell layout of the CFR network control chip mentioned in chapter two is now compared with abutting layouts of the circuit. To avoid the problems of technological differences between the standard cell layout and the proposed three-dimensional cells, the comparison is made in terms of signal lengths rather than estimates of capacitance or delay. For the particular standard cell process used, wiring tracks are $5\mu m$ wide centred on an $11\mu m$ grid. In keeping with the method of recording signal lengths used above, lengths are extracted from the layout data in units of the process design rule λ, which is $3\mu m$. Note that this gives wiring tracks a width of just under 2λ spaced exactly 2λ apart. This is exceptionally well correlated with the three-dimensional design rules assumed for layout of the abutting cells.

Note that to allow direct comparison, the length of each signal extracted from the standard cell layout incorporates a portion equivalent to the half the height of each cell to which the signal is connected. Unlike the library of abutting cells, the standard cells have a range of sizes. For example, a basic inverter is some $7\lambda \times 30\lambda$, while a five input NAND gate is $22\lambda \times 30\lambda$. Again this correlates well with the $27\lambda \times 27\lambda$ for the five input NAND gate cube cell with two connections per face.

8.5.3 Three-dimensional CFR layout

At the top level in the hierarchy of the CFR circuit description there are a small number of blocks of mainly random logic which are assigned similar sized areas in the floor plan. The layout of each of these blocks was formed automatically. It is at this level of granularity in the design that the comparison with equivalent abutting layouts is made. Table 8.4 details the logical sizes of each high level random logic block for both cell libraries.

Note that the design makes use of the flip-flops contained in the standard cell library. Since the abutting cell library contains only simple gates, flip-flops must be synthesised discretely from combinational logic, thereby increasing the node count. For three of the blocks, the abutting node count rises beyond that which the prototype abutment system can handle. In these cases, the logic is further partitioned into two similar sized blocks for which layouts are separately formed. For each pair of layouts, the results are combined and augmented with an estimate of the additional routing required to join the blocks. For each signal which connects two blocks, the estimate used is the sum of the maximum distance between any pair of nodes in

| Block | | Standard cell | | Abutting cell | | Node |
Name	Number	Nodes	Signals	Nodes	Signals	Ratio
TimingS	1	168	198	247	261	1.4
In	2	176	234	338	354	1.9
Transmit	3	203	292	439	478	2.1
Receive	4	227	328	464	510	2.0
WriteRegs	5	233	299	732	694	3.1
ReadRegs	6	264	353	852	797	3.2
Out	7	382	458	748	756	1.9

Table 8.4: CFR logic block sizes in two libraries

both blocks.

8.5.4 Comparison

Figure 8.8 shows the results of the two-dimensional standard cell layout 'SC' together
with the results of abutting cell layouts using different numbers of layers of active
cells 'AL=1', 'AL=2' and 'AL=3'. Each abutting cell layout assumes three additional
layers of passive wiring cells. As before, the data points for the abutting cell layouts
in these graphs are the average of five layout repetitions. However, the data points
for standard cell layouts are from solitary layouts.

First, for the abutting cell layouts the trend as the number of layers increases is in
good agreement with that presented earlier. Therefore the behaviour of the system
with these particular layouts appears to be typical. Second, the quality of the three
active layer abutting cell layouts is generally the same as the standard cell layouts.
Two active layer layouts are slightly worse, while the one active layer layouts are
around 30% worse. There are two notable exceptions within this comparison. First,
the layouts of blocks five and six are rather worse, even for the three layer layouts.
Second, the layout of block one is rather better, with the one layer layout only
slightly worse than the standard cell layout, and both two and three layer layouts
better.

These differences are related, and can be explained by reference to Table 8.4, where
the ratio of the number of nodes in the standard cell and abutting cell libraries is
shown. Blocks five and six contain a number of registers which are constructed from

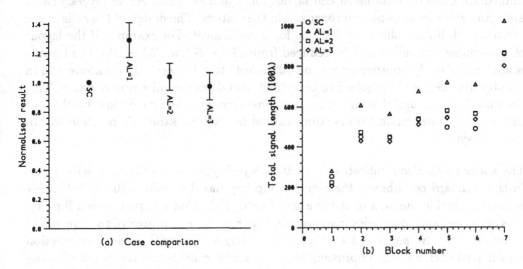

Figure 8.8: CFR block layout

flip-flops in the standard cell layout. In the abutting cell layout, these flip-flops are synthesised from gates, and so the ratio of nodes in the two layouts is high. This results in an unfavourable comparison, since flip-flops are treated more efficiently in the standard cell system. By contrast, block one contains fewer structures which require synthesis in the abutting cell layout, and so the ratio is low. The resulting abutting cell layout compares more favourably.

8.5.5 Discussion

At first sight, the above results may seem disappointing. However, a number of mitigating factors can be identified. First, it must be remembered that the method of forming abutting layouts is a novel technique. Though the layout system presented in chapter six is the result of much experimentation and reworking, it is nevertheless a rudimentary system in comparison with some of the sophisticated methods of conventional layout which have evolved over the years. Considering the two-dimensional behaviour of the system, it could be argued that for such a simple method of automatic layout to produce results within 30% of the tried and tested standard cell layout strategy is encouraging.

Note that any improvements which apply to the abutment system as a whole offer immediate gains over standard cell layout for layout on three active layers. There are many areas for possible improvement in the system. The design of the cells in the abutting cell library offers much scope for improvement. For example, if the layout of two-connection cells could be reduced from $27\lambda \times 27\lambda$ to $25\lambda \times 20\lambda$, the layouts would immediately improve by around 20%. Note that the cells shown above and in chapter five are merely required to be cuboid, and do not require square bases. This need not lose any useful symmetry, since some symmetry is already lost by the fact that up and down vertical connections cannot occupy the same XY position within the cell layout.

The above comparison indicates the inefficiency of synthesising flip-flops with gates. In the standard cell library, the simplest flip-flop has dimensions $50\lambda \times 30\lambda$. This is roughly double the area of the five input gate. Note that the synthesised flip-flop uses six gates, and therefore consumes roughly three times the area of the equivalent standard cell. As suggested earlier, slightly larger cells with greater connection capacity offer significant improvement. It is worth considering the effect of using abutting cells large enough to contain a flip-flop. The detailed design of such cells is beyond the scope of this dissertation. However, it is reasonable to assume that the dimensions of such a cell would be correlated with those of the equivalent standard cell, much the same as for the five input gate. This would result in a cell of size $35\lambda \times 35\lambda$.

Figure 8.9 shows the results of abutting layout using such postulated cells. Note the general improvement, with layouts on two layers now appearing better than the conventional standard cell layout. Furthermore, blocks five and six which previously showed poor abutting layouts are now treated more typically. This is a direct consequence of the use of flip-flop cells. Note that the improvements offered by performing layout utilising flip-flops are tempered by the greater signal lengths between the larger cells.

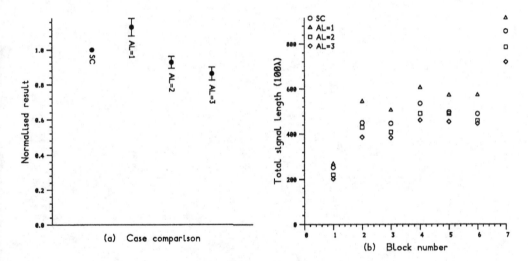

Figure 8.9: CFR block layout utilising flip-flop cells

Chapter 9

Conclusions

9.1 Review

9.1.1 Aims

This dissertation has presented an investigation into three-dimensional integrated circuit layout and cell design. The primary goal of the investigation was to discover the potential benefits of such layout, and to determine whether those benefits justify the considerably more complex and costly techniques of fabrication which are involved.

Similar questions for other difficult fabrication techniques are more readily answered. The cost of techniques used to make smaller transistors is constantly being justified by the denser, faster and more highly integrated circuits and systems which result. It is also the case that such technology does not introduce any fundamentally new layout problems. A more difficult question to answer concerns the value of wafer-scale integration. This is because the benefits are clouded by yield problems, and new layout and fabrication methodologies must be introduced to achieve fault or failure tolerance. The best methods are still to be determined.

The value of three-dimensional integration is a yet more difficult question. The technological difficulties are as apparent as they are abundant, and include yield degradation and thermal stresses during fabrication and heat dissipation and crosstalk during circuit operation. However, the nature of the benefit is not clear. It has been speculated that three-dimensional circuits might be denser and faster, having shorter wiring and offering greater connection capabilities. These benefits are expected because of the inherently richer connection topology which the three-dimensional arrangement of devices offers. Little has been done and less has been published about such speculation.

9.1.2   Preliminary research

As with any new topic of such complexity, an investigation into three-dimensional integrated circuit layout is open-ended. In order to form some context for later developments, a body of preliminary work was presented in the two categories of design and technology.

First, a classification of two-dimensional design methods was introduced. This provided a necessary framework for later discussions about the application of such methods to three-dimensional circuit design. Three-dimensional circuit fabrication techniques were then presented as one of a number of trends in integration. A number of techniques with apparent three-dimensional potential were compared with particular reference to three-dimensional circuit applications. An analysis of the yield of three-dimensional circuits was developed. This was later used to generate tables of yield estimates for three-dimensional circuits.

Next, a classification of three-dimensional structures was devised, based on composition in terms of the number and type of device, wiring and contact layers. Using this classification as a framework, circuit structures and layout techniques were suggested for three-dimensional versions of gate array and standard cell design methodologies. It was then required to conduct some practical experiments in the three-dimensional layout of circuits. This involved the construction of a three-dimensional layout system. It was considered that translating any of the standard methodologies to work in three dimensions would be rather prosaic, and so the primary research effort concentrated on the development of a novel layout technique.

9.1.3   Primary research

The experimental environment was required to provide a ready means of performing circuit layout within a variety of three-dimensional connection topologies. In particular, the principle of layout using maximum cell packing was explicitly embraced.

In this way, the maximum potential of three-dimensional integration can be seen in a way which more conventional layout techniques cannot show.

The principle of the physical abutment of cells of homogeneous size and shape was introduced as a method capable of demonstrating maximum cell packing density. A discussion of tessellating solids on which to model abutting cells was accompanied by examples of circuit layout using such cells, showing the value of this method. The practicality of the method was shown by the design of cuboid cells conforming to postulated design rules for three-dimensional SOI. Symmetric cell layouts were presented as a possible approach to three-dimensional library design. This design exercise provided a necessary injection of technological realism into the later discussions and comparisons.

The process of translating the principles of abutment into a working layout system uncovered a number of properties which such layouts must possess. First, cluster incongruencies must not be allowed to form since these create regions of wiring congestion which can result in routing deadlock. Incongruencies were prevented for cuboid cells by using algorithms to control the shape of cluster growth. Second, signals which are not fully routed must be able to exit from the growing cluster, since such signals are otherwise unroutable. This problem was sub-optimally solved by the simple strategy of guaranteeing that all partially routed signals leave the cluster.

The system was purposefully constructed with a great deal of built-in flexibility. The choices in the placement and routing phases of the abutment process were guided by the evaluation of merit functions. These were designed to reflect the value of each possible placement with the weighted sum of components quantifying the placement and its relationship to the current state of the layout. The weights were determined interactively as were higher level controls over the algorithm behaviour and the layout framework. In this way, the system provided a flexible yet simple approach to forming three-dimensional layouts, and was the main tool in the experimental study which followed.

9.1.4 Experimental results

The experiments with the abutment system were in two distinct phases. In the first phase, the optimum operating conditions of the system were sought. This involved the postulation and evaluation of merit function components and weights. It was found that the simplest of merit functions based only on the number of connections which a possible placement would make was improved by the addition of lookahead and connection length components.

Lookahead was incorporated as a result of investigations into the layout of circuits which have a perfect embedding in the abutting cell framework. The lookahead component encourages the formation of placement patterns for which it is known that there are specific future abutments which would attract a high merit. The use of lookahead improved the otherwise random choice between placements attracting the same merit. The notion of optimum layout which this framework provides was a novel feature, and the ability of the system to find certain perfect embeddings was taken as an indication of sensible behaviour.

In the second phase of experiments, the system was used to investigate the nature of three-dimensional layouts. The detailed design of larger cuboid cells with greater face connectivity was presented. It was found that such cells offered significant layout improvements. This is because the ability to route greater numbers of signals through such cells avoids more circuitous wiring through neighbouring cells. This is despite the disadvantage of the slightly longer wires in larger cells.

The effect on wiring length of introducing reduced vertical separation between layers was found to be broadly as expected. The improvement was attenuated by the inability of the system to treat vertical and horizontal abutments alike, and the relationship between vertical scale, circuit size and layout bounding box was seen to be complex. The effect of using more active layers for layout was central to the dissertation. For the abutment model of layout, it was found that adding more layers of devices was consistent with the expectation of improvement. For sufficiently large circuits, the improvement as the number of layers is increased is sustained. By contrast, the effect of adding wiring only layers was found to be more modest and confined to the addition of a few layers. It can be concluded therefore that the benefit of adding more layers is due to the three-dimensional juxtaposition of cells rather than the implicit introduction of greater wiring capacity.

Finally, a comparison with two-dimensional layout was presented which demonstrated the value of this approach to layout. For the logic blocks of the CFR, a range of two- and three-dimensional abutting layouts using cells with only combinational functionality was shown to be broadly comparable with the conventional standard cell layouts. The greater functionality of the standard cell library was seen to be desirable, and so the benefit of layout using abutting cells with more functionality was postulated. If such cells can be designed within the stipulated dimensions, the two active layer layout of the CFR logic blocks can be expected to show improvement over the standard cell layout.

9.2   Further work

The method of forming layouts by abutting suitably designed cells has been presented as an approach to three-dimensional circuit layout. There are many suggestions for further work, since the topic of three-dimensional layout in general and the method of abutment in particular is new. The suggestions for further work fall into a number of categories.

9.2.1   Cell design

The design of abutting cells is an important issue, not only for the practical purpose of fabricating integrated circuits, but also to judge the efficacy of the method. For a given library of abutting cells, reducing the cell size by better design leads to immediate improvements which can be applied retrospectively to existing layouts. In general, this is not the case for conventional methods, where layout would have to be reconstructed.

A more interesting area of study is the tradeoff between the size and connectivity of cells. For example, consideration could be given to using cells with three connections per face, and so on. For a given circuit, there is some connectivity of cell for which improvement is maximised. There are no gains beyond this point since the active parts of each cell become separated by more and more wiring space which cannot be fully utilised.

The tradeoff between the size and the functionality of cells is more involved, since it relates to the structures required in the circuit. For example, if a design requires a small number of functionally complex nodes which can be synthesised from smaller simpler cells, then there is no advantage in using unnecessarily large cells for the bulk of simple nodes. As the proportion of complex nodes rises, using complex cells becomes an advantage. This relationship could be explored.

For practical purposes, a complete library of abutting cells of given functionality and connection interface must be generated. The large numbers of cells in an abutting library require methods of automated synthesis to be devised. For a range of functions such as NAND gates this can be reduced to essentially a routing problem.

9.2.2   Algorithm improvement

The system was designed to perform layout using any shape of abutting cell. However, the constraints on the shape of cluster growth lead to growth control algorithms specific to cuboid cells. This was unfortunate, since in all other respects the implementation of the system achieved the required generality. The development of growth strategies for other shapes is an interesting question, particularly for hexagonal prism cells since it now appears that cells with greater connectivity are better. The design of a completely general growth strategy for all tessellating cells remains a challenge.

A drawback of constructive techniques is that poor earlier choices cannot be undone. This has been a reason for their decline in popularity. In certain circumstances, the rules about the immutability of placement and routing in abutting layouts can be relaxed. This could be used to develop algorithms to rip up and replace or reroute sections of layout. For placements, cells on the cluster surface which are not the site of segment guarantees can be removed. Indeed, guarantees can be rearranged elsewhere which is itself an area of study. Routing can be ripped up provided that each of the segments formed in the division can be guaranteed.

9.2.3   Broader contexts

An alternative to rip up and redo techniques would be to give the abutment system hints about the relative three-dimensional positions of unplaced nodes. These hints could be loosely determined by iterative techniques. There is a parallel between this approach and the method of placement used for the standard cell layout of the CFR. In that system constructive placement was interspersed with the iterative interchange of the unplaced nodes. A study of the effect of this type of technique on three-dimensional layout where abutment is the constructive element is an interesting prospect.

9.2.4   Other techniques

There is clearly scope for much work investigating the application of traditional methods to three-dimensional layout. This must involve the postulation of a technological framework for the three-dimensional integration together with the reworking of layout algorithms. It is uncertain how such methods will perform, since to do well they must allow the richer topology of three-dimensional device arrangements to be exploited. This topology may only be profitably exploited if the granularity of the access to three-dimensional connection is very low, as in the abutment scheme.

9.3   Summary

The research described in this dissertation has led to the design and implementation of a novel system of automated layout. From the outset, the system was intended to exploit the enhanced connection potential of the three-dimensional arrangement of cells. The system is based on simple heuristics which produce perfect layouts of certain circuits. A high degree of self-consistency in the system indicates that this is a valid layout technique. Furthermore it is practical, as the design of cells exhibiting the required geometric properties has shown. In conclusion, it is suggested that in addition to being a novel vehicle for layout experimentation, the abutment system demonstrates a technique which has practical application in three-dimensional integrated circuit layout.

Appendix A

Layout Editor Configuration

The configuration file of the Qudos Layout Editor describes routable layers such as metal and polysilicon and via layers which describe the relationship between routable layers. For three-dimensional CMOS SOI design rules, a vertical connection is described by a metal layer with no contact overlap. The contact overlap will be provided on the planar metal layer to which the vertical metal layer connects. The structure of the layers is shown in Figure A.1. The layer 'Dummy' avoids a limitation of the system, and is introduced to maintain full design rule checking. The corresponding configuration file is included below.

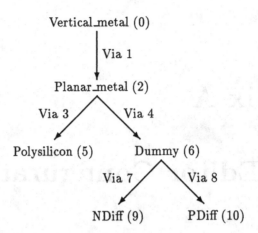

Figure A.1: The relationship between layers in a configuration file for a three-dimensional CMOS SOI process

```
process 3D_SOI;

AUTO_POWER;
FULL_CUSTOM;
number_of_layers=11;  (* including 3 DUMMY *)
base_gridsize=100;
grid_multiplier=2;    (* use a 2um grid *)

LAYER Vertical_metal 0 metal;
  routable;
  minrad=100;
  mingap=400;
  via_below=1;
  via_border_below=0;
  colours(White,*,*,*,*,*);
END;

LAYER Via 1 via;
  minrad=100;
  mingap=400;
  route_above=0;
  route_below=2;
  colours(Black,*,*,*,*,*);
END;

LAYER Planar_metal 2 metal;
```

```
      routable;
      minrad=100;
      mingap=200;
      via_above=1;
      via_border_above=200; (* oversized overlap *)
      via_below=3;
      alternative_via_below=4;
      via_border_below=100; (* ordinary overlap *)
      colours(Blue,*,*,*,*,*);
END;

LAYER Via 3 via;
      minrad=100;
      mingap=0;
      route_above=2;
      route_below=5;
      colours(Black,*,*,*,*,*);
END;

LAYER Via 4 via;
      minrad=100;
      mingap=0;
      route_above=2;
      route_below=6;
      colours(Black,*,*,*,*,*);
END;
```

```
LAYER Polysilicon 5 poly;
  routable;
  minrad=100;
  mingap=200;
  via_above=3;
  colours(Magenta,*,*,*,*,*);
END;

LAYER Dummy 6 metal;
  DUMMY;
  minrad=100;
  mingap=200;
  via_above=4;
  via_below=7;
  alternative_via_below=8;
  colours(White,*,*,*,*,*);
END;

LAYER Via 7 via;
  DUMMY;
  minrad=100;
  mingap=0;
  route_above=6;
  route_below=9;
  colours(Black,*,*,*,*,*);
END;

LAYER Via 8 via;
  DUMMY;
  minrad=100;
  mingap=0;
  route_above=6;
  route_below=10;
  colours(Black,*,*,*,*,*);
END;

LAYER NDiff 9 ndiff;
  routable;
  minrad=100;
  mingap=300;
  via_above=7;
  via_border_above=100;
  colours(Green,*,*,*,*,*);
END;

LAYER PDiff 10 pdiff;
  routable;
  minrad=100;
```

```
    mingap=300;
    via_above=8;
    via_border_above=100;
    colours(Yellow,*,*,*,*,*);
END;
```

Appendix B

Layout System Data Structures

The layout system was written in Modula-2 [Wirth 80].

Fields involved in circuit representation are commented with the letter C.
Fields involved in layout representation are commented with the letter L.

```
(* Imports *)

FROM names    IMPORT Name;
FROM geometry IMPORT IVec, RVec;

(*  References *)

Node = POINTER TO NodeRecord;
Signal = POINTER TO SignalRecord;
Contact = POINTER TO ContactRecord;
Cell = POINTER TO CellRecord;
Port = POINTER TO PortRecord;
Segment = POINTER TO SegmentRecord;
Perm = POINTER TO PermRecord;

(* Types *)

Mode = (Input, Output);
Class = (Active, Passive);
Wire = [0..MaxWires];
Orientation = [0..MaxOrientations];
Type = (None, Free, Route, Logic, Through);
Interface = ARRAY Wire OF Port;
Abutment = ARRAY Wire OF
          RECORD
```

```
    cell: Cell;
    edge: Wire
END;
```

```
(* Circuit representations *)

NodeRecord = RECORD
  name:      Name;        (* C: an encoded name                      *)
  parent:    Node;        (* C: a link back up the hierarchy         *)
  next:      Node;        (* C: a link in list of siblings           *)
  CASE type: CARDINAL OF
  HighLevel:
    child:   Node;        (* C: a link to sub-structure              *)
    signal:  Signal;      (* C: a list of local signals              *)
  ELSE
    contact: Contact;     (* C: the connections to signals           *)
    cell:    Cell;        (* L: a position in the layout             *)
    select:  Node;        (* L: a link to list of selected nodes     *)
  END;
END;

SignalRecord = RECORD
  name:     Name;         (* C: an encoded name                      *)
  node:     Node;         (* C: the node where signal was declared   *)
  next:     Signal;       (* C: a link in a list of siblings         *)
  contact:  Contact;      (* C: the connections to nodes             *)
  segment:  Segment;      (* L: all ports which refer to the signal  *)
END;

ContactRecord = RECORD
  node:          Node;    (* C node involved in connection           *)
  signal:        Signal;  (* C signal involved in connection         *)
  mode:          Mode;    (* C contact mode between signal and node  *)
  nextnode,               (* C list of nodes which signal connects   *)
  nextsignal:    Contact; (* C list of signals which node connects   *)
END;
```

```
(* Layout representations *)

CellRecord = RECORD
  class:     Class;       (* L class of cell which may be put here *)
  virtual:   IVec;        (* L virtual coordinate of the cell      *)
  real:      RVec;        (* L real coordinate of the cell         *)
  abutment:  Abutment ;   (* L abutting vertices and edges         *)
  orient:    Orientation; (* L orientation of cell at this cell    *)
  used:      BOOLEAN;     (* L is cell used?                       *)
  usable:    BOOLEAN;     (* L is cell usable?                     *)
  interface: Interface;   (* L interface of ports to neighbours    *)
  capacity:  Wire;        (* L spare capacity of this cell         *)
  node:      Node;        (* L node occupying this cell            *)
  here:      Port;        (* L list of all ports at the cell       *)
  enter:     Wire;        (* L attempted route enters here         *)
  route:     Port;        (* L identity of attempted route         *)
END;

PortRecord = RECORD
  next:      Port;        (* L link of ports at the same cell       *)
  type:      Type;        (* L nature of connection                 *)
  cell:      Cell;        (* L location of this port                *)
  segment:   Segment;     (* L segment for type logic or wire       *)
  reserved:  INTEGER;     (* L number of reserved interface entries *)
  assigned:  INTEGER;     (* L number of assigned interface entries *)
  chain:     Port;        (* L link of ports in the same segment    *)
  span:      RVec;        (* L distance from nearest contact        *)
END;

SegmentRecord = RECORD
  next:   Segment;   (* L link to other segments of the signal *)
  signal: Signal;    (* L identity of signal                   *)
  chain:  Port;      (* L list of ports for this segment       *)
END;

PermRecord = RECORD
  interface: Interface;            (* L possible interface      *)
  count:     ARRAY Type OF INTEGER;(* L count of each port type *)
  next:      Perm;                 (* L link in list of perms   *)
END;
```

Appendix C

Cell Description Rules

C.1 Cube

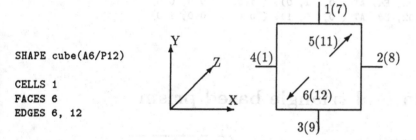

SHAPE cube(A6/P12)

CELLS 1
FACES 6
EDGES 6, 12

ACTIVE

```
(01, E1)  ABUTS (01, E3)  AT (0, 1, 0), (0.0, 1.0, 0.0)
(01, E2)  ABUTS (01, E4)  AT (1, 0, 0), (1.0, 0.0, 0.0)
(01, E5)  ABUTS (01, E6)  AT (0, 0, 1), (0.0, 0.0, 1.0)
```

PASSIVE

```
(01, E7)  ABUTS (01, E9)  AT (0, 1, 0), (0.0, 1.0, 0.0)
(01, E8)  ABUTS (01, E10) AT (1, 0, 0), (1.0, 0.0, 0.0)
(01, E11) ABUTS (01, E12) AT (0, 0, 1), (0.0, 0.0, 1.0)
```

C.2   Hexagon based prism

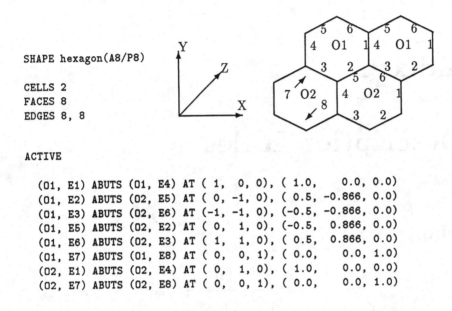

SHAPE hexagon(A8/P8)

CELLS 2
FACES 8
EDGES 8, 8

ACTIVE

```
(01, E1) ABUTS (01, E4) AT ( 1,  0, 0), ( 1.0,   0.0, 0.0)
(01, E2) ABUTS (02, E5) AT ( 0, -1, 0), ( 0.5, -0.866, 0.0)
(01, E3) ABUTS (02, E6) AT (-1, -1, 0), (-0.5, -0.866, 0.0)
(01, E5) ABUTS (02, E2) AT ( 0,  1, 0), (-0.5,  0.866, 0.0)
(01, E6) ABUTS (02, E3) AT ( 1,  1, 0), ( 0.5,  0.866, 0.0)
(01, E7) ABUTS (01, E8) AT ( 0,  0, 1), ( 0.0,   0.0, 1.0)
(02, E1) ABUTS (02, E4) AT ( 0,  1, 0), ( 1.0,   0.0, 0.0)
(02, E7) ABUTS (02, E8) AT ( 0,  0, 1), ( 0.0,   0.0, 1.0)
```

C.3   Equilateral triangle based prism

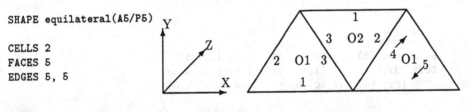

SHAPE equilateral(A5/P5)

CELLS 2
FACES 5
EDGES 5, 5

ACTIVE

```
(01, E1) ABUTS (02, E1) AT ( 0, -1, 0), ( 0.0,  -1.0, 0.0)
(01, E2) ABUTS (02, E2) AT (-1,  0, 0), (-0.5, 0.866, 0.0)
(01, E3) ABUTS (02, E3) AT ( 1,  0, 0), ( 0.5, 0.866, 0.0)
(01, E4) ABUTS (01, E5) AT ( 0,  0, 1), ( 0.0,   0.0, 1.0)
(02, E4) ABUTS (02, E5) AT ( 0,  0, 1), ( 0.0,   0.0, 1.0)
```

Appendix D

Circuits

D.1 Configuration circuits

D.2 Evaluation circuits

Circuit	Nodes	Signals	Signals per node	Nodes per signal
dtype	6	6	2.6	2.6
demult2	12	8	1.8	2.7
shift2	15	14	2.7	2.9
rippadd2	22	14	2.2	3.5
shift4	27	26	2.9	3.0
Local1	39	27	1.6	2.3
shift8	51	50	3.0	3.1
demult4	72	56	2.3	3.0
arbiter	75	74	3.1	3.1
Refresh1	89	81	2.9	3.2
shift16	99	98	3.1	3.1
ECL(C)	106	100	2.8	2.9
wcfr	123	122	3.1	3.1
demult5	138	106	2.6	3.4
ECL(B)	145	139	2.8	2.9
cprx	147	146	3.1	3.1
cptx1	162	145	2.7	3.0
cmain	171	170	3.1	3.1
shift32	195	194	3.1	3.1
ECL(A)	205	198	2.8	3.0

Table D.1: Twenty circuits used during system configuration

Circuit	Nodes	Signals	Signals per node	Nodes per signal
adder	8	10	2.5	2.0
srlatch	8	12	3.0	2.0
demult3	22	14	2.2	3.5
ripadd4	33	41	3.7	3.0
readcntrl	58	65	3.2	2.9
parity8	65	81	3.8	3.0
execute	75	74	3.0	3.1
transtime	109	113	3.2	3.0
fetch	120	122	3.1	3.1
ripadd16	129	161	3.8	3.0
traffic	147	146	3.1	3.1
barrel	171	170	3.1	3.1
tapectrl	249	229	2.1	2.3
display	262	241	2.3	2.5
cmain	263	253	2.1	2.2
multiply	285	241	2.7	3.1
wmain	337	320	2.7	2.8
Refresh	353	316	2.7	3.0
VideoC	405	354	2.5	2.8
ECL	407	392	2.9	3.0

Table D.2: Twenty additional circuits used during layout evaluation

References

The pages on which references are cited appear in parentheses after each reference.

[Atherton 83] W.A. Atherton. *From Compass to Computer*. The Macmillan Press, London and Basingstoke, 1983.

[Aubusson 78] R.C. Aubusson and I. Catt. Wafer-scale integration - a fault-tolerant procedure. *IEEE Journal of Solid-State Circuits*, 13(3):339–344, June 1978.

[Augarten 83] S. Augarten. *State of The Art*. Ticknor and Fields, New Haven and New York, 1983.

[Braun 82] E. Braun and S. Macdonald. *Revolution in Miniature*. Cambridge University Press, 1982.

[Broadbent 88] E.K. Broadbent, J.M. Flanner, W.G.M. Van Den Hoek, and I. Connick. High-density high-reliability tungsten interconnection by filled interconnect groove metallisation. *IEEE Transactions on Electron Devices*, 35(7):952–956, July 1988.

[Brown 87] D.M. Brown, B. Gorowitz, P. Piacente, R. Saia, R. Wilson, and D. Woodruff. Selective cvd tungsten via plugs for multilevel metallisation. *IEEE Electron Device Letters*, 8(2):55–57, 1987.

[Bruer 77] M.A. Bruer and A.D. Friedman. *Diagnosis and Reliable Design of Digital Systems*. Computer Science Press, 1977.

[Buric 83] M.R. Buric, C. Christensen, and T.G. Matheson. Plex: Automatically generated computer layouts. In *Proceedings International Conference on Computer Design*, pages 181–184, October 1983.

[Burstein 83] M. Burstein and R. Pelavin. Hierarchical channel router. *Integration; The VLSI Journal*, 1(1):21–38, 1983.

193

[Calder 85] I.D. Calder and H.M. Naguib. Activation of polysilicon connections by selective cw laser annealing. *IEEE Electron Device Letters*, 6(10):557–559, October 1985.

[Camposano 89] R. Camposano and W. Rosenstiel. Synthesising circuits from behavioural descriptions. *IEEE Transactions on Computer Aided Design*, 8(2):171–180, February 1989.

[Carlson 86] R.O. Carlson and C.A. Neugebauer. Future trends in wafer scale integration. *Proceedings of the IEEE*, 74(12):1741–1752, December 1986.

[Colinge 86] J-P. Colinge. Half-micrometre-base lateral bipolar transistors made in thin silicon-on-insulator films. *Electronics Letters*, 22(17):886–887, August 1986.

[Denyer 82] P. Denyer, D. Renshaw, and N. Bergmann. A silicon compiler for vlsi signal processors. In *Proceedings of the European Solid State Circuits Conference*, 1982.

[Dukes 61] J.M.C. Dukes. *Printed Circuits*. Macdonald and Co., 1961.

[Dummer 83] G.W.A. Dummer. *Electronic Inventions and Discoveries*. Pergamon, 1983.

[Dunlop 80] A. Dunlop. Slim — the translation of symbolic layouts into mask data. In *Proceedings 17th ACM/IEEE Design Automation Conference*, pages 595–602, June 1980.

[Dunlop 85] A.E. Dunlop and B.W. Kernighan. A procedure for placement of standard-cell vlsi circuits. *IEEE Transactions on Computer Aided Design*, 4(1):92–98, January 1985.

[Eichelberger 77] E.B. Eichelberger and T.W. Williams. A logic design structure for lsi testing. In *Proceedings 14th ACM/IEEE Design Automation Conference*, pages 462–468, June 1977.

[El Ziq 83] Y.M. El-Ziq. S^3: Vlsi self-test using signature analysis and scan path techniques. In *IEEE International Conference on Computer Aided Design*, pages 73–76, 1983.

[Electronics 85a] R. Gallagher. Thomson-csf/cnet team for soi. *Electronics Week*, pages 26–27, March 1985.

[Electronics 85b] K. Smith. Britons seek tolerant chips. *Electronics Week*, pages 20–24, February 1985.

[ESPRIT 86] ESPRIT Project 245. 3d-soi design options study. Technical report, National Microelectronics Research Centre, University College, Cork, Ireland, February 1986.

[Fairbairn 78] D.G. Fairbairn and J.A. Rowson. Icarus: An interactive integrated circuit layout program. In *Proceedings 15th ACM/IEEE Design Automation Conference*, pages 210–228, June 1978.

[Fichtner 82] W. Fichtner, R.K. Watts, D.B. Fraser, R.L.Johnstone, and S.M. Sze. 0.15-μm channel length mosfets fabricated using e-beam lithography. *IEEE Electron Device Letters*, 3(12):412, 1982.

[Friedrich 89] J.A. Friedrich and G.W. Neudeck. Interface characterisation of silicon epitaxial lateral growth over existing SiO_2 for three-dimensional cmos structures. *IEEE Electron Device Letters*, 10(4):144–146, April 1989.

[Fujii 88] E. Fujii, K. Senda, F. Emoto, and Y. Hiroshima. A cpd image sensor with an soi structure. *IEEE Transactions on Electron Devices*, 35(5):642–645, May 1988.

[Gandemer 88] S. Gandemer, B.C. Tremintin, and J-J. Charlot. Critical area and critical levels calculation in i.c. yield modelling. *IEEE Transactions on Electron Devices*, 35(2):158–166, February 1988.

[Geis 86] M.W. Geis, C.K. Chen, R.W. Mountain, N.P. Economou, W.T. Lindley, and P.L. Hower. Use of zone-melting recrystallisation to fabricate a three-dimensional structure incorporating power bipolar and field-effect transistors. *IEEE Electron Device Letters*, 7(1):41–43, January 1986.

[Gibbons 80] J.F. Gibbons and K.F. Lee. One-gate-wide cmos inverter on laser-recrystallised polysilicon. *IEEE Electron Device Letters*, 1(6):117–118, June 1980.

[Goldstein 79] L.H. Goldstein. Controllability/observability analysis of digital circuits. *IEEE Transactions on Circuits and Systems*, 26(9), 1979.

[Goodman 84] J.W. Goodman, F.J. Leonberger, S-Y. Kung, and R.A. Athale. Optical interconnections for vlsi systems. *Proceedings of the IEEE*, 72(7):850–866, 1984.

[Grinberg 84] J. Grinberg, G.R. Nudd, and R.D. Etchells. A cellular vlsi architecture. *IEEE Transactions on Computers*, 33(1):69–81, January 1984.

[Gunrath 89] B. Gunrath and N.N. Biswas. An algorithm for multiple output minimisation. *IEEE Transactions on Computer Aided Design*, 8(9):1007–1014, September 1989.

[Hirashita 89] N. Hirashita, T. Katoh, and H. Onoda. Si-gate cmos devices on a Si lateral solid-phase epitaxial layer. *IEEE Transactions on Electron Devices*, 36(3):548–552, March 1989.

[Hite 85] L.R. Hite, R. Sundaresan, S.D.S Malhi, H.W. Lam, A.H. Shah, R.K. Hester, and P.K. Chaterjee. Process and performance comparison of an 8k × 8-bit sram in three stacked cmos technologies. *IEEE Electron Device Letters*, 6(10):548–550, October 1985.

[Hoefflinger 84] B. Hoefflinger, S.T. Liu, and B. Vajdic. A three-dimensional cmos design methodology. *IEEE Transactions on Electron Devices*, 31(2):171–173, February 1984.

[Hofmann 83] M. Hofmann and V. Lauther. Hex: An instruction driven approach to feature extraction. In *Proceedings 20th ACM/IEEE Design Automation Conference*, pages 331–336, June 1983.

[Hopper 84] G.F. Hopper, J.R. Davis, R.A. McMahon, and H. Ahmed. Silicon-on-insulator cmos transistors in dual electron beam recrystallised polysilicon. *Electronics Letters*, 20(12):500–501, June 1984.

[Hopper 88] A. Hopper and R.M. Needham. The cambridge fast ring networking system. *IEEE Transactions on Computers*, 37(10), October 1988.

[Hotta 88] T. Hotta, K. Kurita, H. Maejima, M. Iwamura, S. Tanaka, T. Bandoh, T. Yamauchi, and A. Hotta. 1.3-μm cmos/bipolar standard cell library for vlsi computers. *IEEE Journal of Solid-State Circuits*, 23(2):500–505, April 1988.

[Inou 86] Y. Inou, K. Sugahara, S. Kusunoki, M. Nakaya, T. Nishimura, Y. Horiba, Y. Akasaka, and H. Nakata. A three-dimensional static ram. *IEEE Electron Device Letters*, 7(5):327–329, May 1986.

[Johannsen 78] D. Johannsen. Bristle blocks: A silicon compiler. In *Proceedings 15th ACM/IEEE Design Automation Conference*, pages 310–313, June 1978.

[Kawamura 83] S. Kawamura, N. Sasaki, T. Iwai, M. Nakano, and M. Takagi. Three-dimensional cmos ics fabricated by using beam recrystallisation. *IEEE Electron Device Letters*, 4(10):366–368, October 1983.

[Kawamura 84a] S. Kawamura, N. Sasaki, T. Iwai, R. Mukai, M. Nakano, and M. Takagi. 3-dimensional gate array with vertically stacked dual soi/cmos structure fabricated by beam recrystallisation. In *VLSI Symposium*, September 1984.

[Kawamura 84b] S. Kawamura, N. Sasaki, T. Iwai, R. Mukai, M. Nakano, and M. Takagi. Electrical characteristics of three-dimensional soi/cmos ics. *IEEE Electron Device Letters*, 5(7):248–250, July 1984.

[Kim 85] M.J. Kim, D.M. Brown, S.S. Cohen, P. Piacente, and B. Gorowitz. Mo/TiW contact for vlsi applications. *IEEE Transactions on Electron Devices*, 32(8):1328–1333, August 1985.

[Kobayashi 89] Y. Kobayashi, K. Asayama, M. Oohayashi, R. Hori, G. Kitsukawa, and K. Itoh. Bipolar cmos-merged technology for a high-speed 1-Mbit dram. *IEEE Transactions on Electron Devices*, 36(4):706–711, April 1989.

[Komano 88] H. Komano, Y. Ohmura, and T. Takigawa. Focused-ion-beam fuse cutting for redundancy technology. *IEEE Transactions on Electron Devices*, 35(7):899–903, July 1988.

[Kowalsky 83] T.J. Kowalsky and D.E. Thomas. The vlsi design automation assistant: Prototype system. In *Proceedings 20th ACM/IEEE Design Automation Conference*, 1983.

[Kwasnick 88] R.F. Kwasnick, E.B. Kaminsky, P.A. Frank, G.A. Franz, K.J. Polasko, R.j. Saia, and T.B. Gorczya. An investigation of molybdenum gate for submicrometer cmos. *IEEE Transactions on Electron Devices*, 35(9):1432–1437, September 1988.

[Kwon 87] O.K. Kwon, B.W. Langley, R.F.W. Pease, and M.R. Beasley. Superconductors as very high-speed system-level interconnects. *IEEE Electron Device Letters*, 8(12):582–585, December 1987.

[Lai 86] F-S.J. Lai, L.K. Wang, Y. Taur, J.Y-C. Sun, K.E. Petrillo, S.K. Chicotka, E.J. Petrillo, M.R. Polcari, T.K. Bucelot, and D.S. Zicherman. A highly latchup-immune 1-μm cmos technology fabricated with 1-MeV ion implantation and self-aligned $TiSi_2$. *IEEE Transactions on Electron Devices*, 33(9):1309–1319, September 1986.

[Lasky 86] J.B. Lasky. Wafer bonding for silicon-on-insulator technologies. *Applied Physics Letters*, 48(1):78–80, January 1986.

[Lattice 82] Lattice Logic Ltd. *Designing with Gate Arrays*. Edinburgh, 3.2 edition, 1982.

[Lee 61] C.Y. Lee. An algorithm for path connection and its applications. *IRE Transactions on Electronic Computers*, pages 346–365, September 1961.

[Lee 79] K.F. Lee, J.F. Gibbons, and T.I. Kamins. Thin film mosfets fabricated in laser-annealed polycrystalline silicon. *Applied Physics Letters*, 33:775–779, 1979.

[Leighton 82] F.T. Leighton. A layout strategy for vlsi which is provably good. In *Proceedings 14th ACM Symposium on Theory of Computing*, pages 85–89, 1982.

[Leighton 83] F.T. Leighton and A.L. Rosenberg. Automatic generation of three-dimensional circuit layouts. In *IEEE International Conference on Computer Design: VLSI in Computers*, pages 633–636, 1983.

[Leighton 85] F.T. Leighton and A.L. Rosenberg. Three-dimensional circuit layouts. Technical report, Massachusetts Institute of Technology, 1985.

[Manasevit 64] H.M. Manasevit and W.I. Simpson. Single crystal silicon on a sapphire substrate. *Journal of Applied Physics*, 35:1349–1351, 1964.

[Mathewson 89] A. Mathewson, April 1989. Private communication.

[Mead 80] C.A. Mead and L.A. Conway. *Introduction to VLSI Systems*. Addison-Wesley Publishing Company, 1980.

[Mikaye 87] M. Mikaye, T. Kobayashi, K. Deguchi, M. Kimizuka, S. Horiguchi, and K. Kiuchi. Subhalf-micrometer p-channel mosfets with 3.5nm gate oxide fabricated using X-ray lithography. *IEEE Electron Device Letters*, 8(6):266–268, June 1987.

[Moriya 83] T. Moriya, S. Shima, Y. Hazuki, M. Chiba, and M. Kashawagi. A planar metallisation process — its application to tri-level aluminium interconnections. *IEDM Technical Digest*, pages 550–553, December 1983.

[Murphy 64] B.T. Murphy. Cost-size optima of monolithic integrated circuits. *Proceedings IEEE*, 52:1537–1545, 1964.

[Nage 75] L.W. Nagel. Spice2: A computer program to simulate semiconductor circuits. Technical report, University of California, Berkley, CA, May 1975.

[Needham 82] R.M. Needham and A.J. Herbert. *The Cambridge Distributed System*. Addison-Wesley, 1982.

[Newton 80] A.R. Newton. Timing, logic and mixed-mode simulation for large mos integrated circuits. In *NATO Advanced Study Institute on Computer Design Aids for VLSI Circuits*, SOGESTA, Urbino, Italy, 1980.

[Newton 85] A.R. Newton. Techniques for logic synthesis. In *Proceedings International Conference on VLSI*, 1985.

[O 88] K. O, H-S. Lee, R. Reif, and W. Frank. A 2-μm process utilising selective epitaxy. *IEEE Electron Device Letters*, 9(11):567–569, November 1988.

[Oktay 82] S. Oktay and C. Kammerer. A conduction cooled module for high performance lsi devices. *IBM Journal of Research and Development*, 26(1):55–66, January 1982.

[Onoda 87] H. Onoda, M. Sasaki, T. Katoh, and N. Hirashita. Si-gate cmos devices on a Si/CaF$_2$/Si structure. *IEEE Transactions on Electron Devices*, 34(11):2280–2285, November 1987.

[Preparata 82] F.P. Preparata. Three layers are enough. In *Proceedings 19th ACM/IEEE Design Automation Conference*, pages 350–357, June 1982.

[Qudos 88] *Full Custom ALED Users Manual*, 1988.

[Rivest 82] R.L. Rivest and C.M. Fiduccia. A "greedy" channel router. In *Proceedings 19th ACM/IEEE Design Automation Conference*, pages 418–424, June 1982.

[Robinson 82] P. Robinson and J. Dion. Design aids for uncommitted logic arrays. In *2nd International Conference on Semi-custom ICs*, November 1982.

[Rosenberg 83] A.L. Rosenberg. Three-dimensional vlsi: A case study. *Journal of the Association for Computing Machinery*, 30(3):397–416, July 1983.

[Sasaki 86] S. Sasaki and T. Kishimoto. Optimal structure for microgrooved cooling fin for high-power lsi devices. *Electronics Letters*, 22(25):1332–1333, December 1986.

[Shichijo 88] H. Shichijo, R.J. Mayati, and A.H. Taddiken. Co-integration of GaAs mesfet and Si cmos circuits. *IEEE Electron Device Letters*, 9(9):444–446, September 1988.

[Spickelmier 83] R.L. Spickelmier and A.R. Newton. Wombat: A new netlist comparison program. In *Proceedings IEEE International Conference on CAD*, pages 170–171, September 1983.

[Spielberger 84] R.K. Spielberger, C.D. Huang, W.H. Nunne, A.H. Mones, D.L. Fett, and F.L. Hampton. Silicon-on-silicon packaging. *IEEE Transactions on Components, Hybrids, and Manufacturing Technology*, 7(2):193–196, June 1984.

[Stapper 73] C.H. Stapper. Defect density distribution for lsi yield calculations. *IEEE Transactions on Electron Devices*, 20:655–657, July 1973.

[Stavridou 88] V. Stavridou, H. Barringer, and D.A. Edwards. Formal specification and verification of hardware: A comparative study. In *Proceedings 25th ACM/IEEE Design Automation Conference*, June 1988.

[Sturm 84] J.C. Sturm, M.D. Giles, and J.F. Gibbons. A three-dimensional folded dynamic ram in beam-recrystallised polysilicon. *IEEE Electron Device Letters*, 5(5):151–153, May 1984.

[Sturm 85] J.C. Sturm and J.F. Gibbons. Vertical bipolar transistors in laser-recrystallised polysilicon. *IEEE Electron Device Letters*, 6(8):400–402, August 1985.

[Sugahara 86] K. Sugahara, T. Nishimura, S. Kusunoki, and H. Nakata. Soi/soi/bulk-si triple level structure for three-dimensional devices. *IEEE Electron Device Letters*, 7(3):193–195, March 1986.

[Sugiura 85] S. Sugiura, T. Yoshida, Y. Kaneko, K. Shono, and D.J. Dumin. Mos integrated circuits fabricated on multilayer heteroepitaxial silicon-on-insulator structures for applications to 3-d integrated circuits. *IEEE Transactions on Electron Devices*, 32(11):2307–2313, November 1985.

[Terada 87] K. Terada, S. Kurosawa, and T. Takeshima. A new soft-error-immune dram cell using a stacked cmos structure. *IEEE Transactions on Electron Devices*, 34(6):1268–1372, June 1987.

[Thompson 79] C.D. Thompson. Area-time complexity for vlsi. In *Proceedings 11th ACM Symposium on Theory of Computing*, pages 81–88, 1979.

[Tsai 88] H-H. Tsai, S-M. Chen, H-B. Chen, and C-Y. Wu. An evaluation of furox isolation technology for vlsi/nmosfet fabrication. *IEEE Transactions on Electron Devices*, 35(3):275–284, March 1988.

[Tsaur 82] B.Y. Tsaur, J.C.C. Fan, R.L. Chapman, M.W. Geis, D.J. Silversmith, and R.W. Mountain. Soi/cmos circuits fabricated in zone-melting recrystallised Si films on SiO_2-coated Si substrates. *IEEE Electron Device Letters*, 3(12):398–401, December 1982.

[Tsaur 84] B-Y. Tsaur, R.W. Mountain, C.K. Chen, and J.C.C. Fan. Merged cmos/bipolar technologies utilising zone-melting recrystallised soi films. *IEEE Electron Device Letters*, 5(11):461–463, November 1984.

[Tsutsui 87] K. Tsutsui, T. Nakazawa, T. Asano, H. Ishiwara, and S. Furukawa. Mesfets on a GaAs-on-insulator structure. *IEEE Electron Device Letters*, 8(6):277–279, June 1987.

[Tuckerman 81] D.B. Tuckerman and R.F.W. Pease. High-performance heat sinking for vlsi. *IEEE Electron Device Letters*, 2(5):126–129, May 1981.

[Unagami 88] T. Unagami and O. Kogure. High-voltage tft fabricated in re-crystallised polycrystalline silicon. *IEEE Transactions on Electron Devices*, 35(3):314–319, March 1988.

[Washio 87] K. Washio, Y. Okada, and T. Okabe. Cmos-compatible bipolar and I^2L technology using three-level epitaxial layers for analog/digital vlsi. *IEEE Transactions on Electron Devices*, 34(8):1708–1712, August 1987.

[Weste 85] N. Weste and K. Eshraghian. *Principles of CMOS VLSI Design*. Addison-Wesley Publishing Company, 1985.

[Wirth 80] N. Wirth. Modula-2. Technical Report 36, ETH, Institut fur Informatik, ETH, CH-8092 Zürich, March 1980.

[Ying 89] C-S. Ying and J.S-L. Wong. An analytical approach to floorplanning for hierarchical building blocks layout. *IEEE Transactions on Computer Aided Design*, 8(4):420–425, April 1989.

Index